HOW TO GET YOUR OWN PATENT

ROBERT O. RICHARDSON

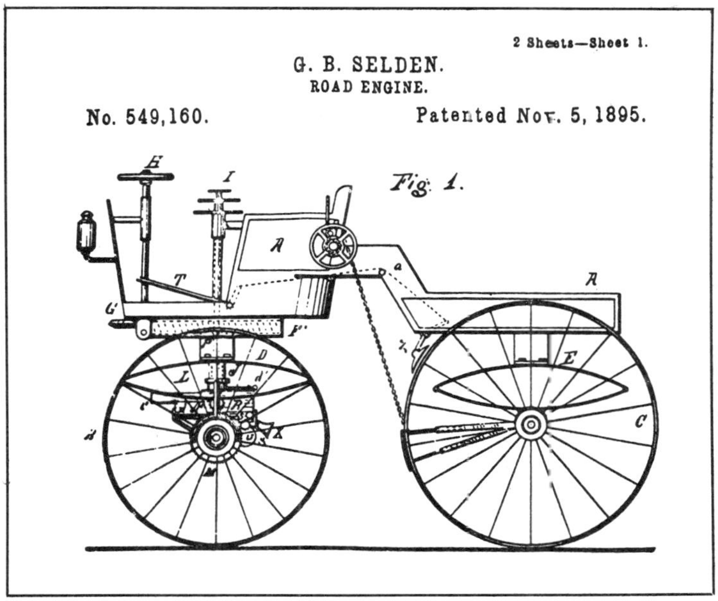

Sterling Publishing Co., Inc. New York
Oak Tree Press Co., Ltd. London & Sydney

About the Author

Robert O. Richardson, a former Patent Office Examiner, holds a Doctor of Laws degree from The George Washington University and has been a registered patent attorney for over 25 years. He has represented the U.S. Navy, U.S. Army, and a number of corporations, as well as a host of individual inventors. All told, he counts over 500 successful patent prosecutions to his credit.

Library of Congress Cataloging in Publication Data

Richardson, Robert O.
How to get your own patent.

Includes index.
1. Patent laws and legislation—United States—Popular works. I. Title.
KF3114.6.R5 346.7304′86 80-54340
ISBN 0-8069-5564-3 AACR2
ISBN 0-8069-5565-1 (lib. bdg.)
ISBN 0-8069-8990-4 (pbk.)

Oak Tree ISBN 7061-2805-2

Published by Sterling Publishing Co., Inc.
Two Park Avenue, New York, N.Y. 10016
Manufactured in the United States of America

Contents

Foreword

This book is for innovative people with imagination who seek to improve things. They may or may not be inventors. I tell them how to get their own patents. For those who elect to have registered patent attorneys or agents help them get their patents, I explain how it is done and how the inventor can save his attorney time, and himself money, by being knowledgeable in the skill of acquiring patents. I have no intention of converting an engineer into a patent agent or a lawyer into a patent attorney. However, the successful strategies I disclose will be of definite value to both, as well as to the inventor who wishes to get his own patent.

Questions and Answers about Patents

Q *What is a patent?*

A A patent is a grant issued by the U.S. government giving an inventor the right to exclude all others from making, using, or selling his invention within the United States, its territories, and possessions. In return, he must disclose his invention sufficiently for one skilled in the art to practice it.

Q *What is the difference between a patent, copyright, and trademark?*

A A patent gives the owner the right to prevent others from practicing his invention. A copyright protects the literary, dramatic, musical, and artistic works of an author. It goes to the form of expression rather than to the subject matter. It only prevents copying but does not prevent others from doing the same thing without copying. Mere ideas, plans, and formulae are not protected. Copyrights are registered in the Copyright Office in the Library of Congress. Notice of copyright is applied to the first edition with an encircled R, date, and name of the owner, even before actual registration is made. You can obtain other information about copyrights by writing to the Register of Copyrights, Library of

Q ***What is the difference between a patent, copyright, and trademark? (cont.)***

Congress, Washington, D.C. 20540. A trademark relates to any word, name, symbol, or device that is used in trade with goods to indicate the source or origin of the goods and to distinguish them from the goods of others. Trademark rights prevent others from using a confusingly similar mark but do not prevent others from making or selling the same goods under another mark.

Q ***For how long is a patent granted?***

A Seventeen years from the date on which it is issued, except for patents on ornamental designs, which are granted for terms of 3½, 7, or 14 years.

Q ***Does the patentee continue to have any control over the use of the invention after his patent expires?***

A No; anyone has the free right to use an invention covered in an expired patent, so long as he does not use features covered in other unexpired patents in doing so.

Q ***On what subject matter may a patent be granted?***

A A patent may be granted to the inventor or discoverer of any new and useful process, machine, manufacture, or composition of matter, or any new and useful improvement thereof, or on any distinct and new variety of plant, other than a tuber-propagated plant, which is asexually reproduced, or on any new, original, and ornamental design for an article of manufacture.

Q ***On what subject matter may a patent not be granted?***

A A patent may not be granted on a useless device, on printed matter, on a method of doing business, on an improvement in a device that would be obvious to a person skilled in the art, or on a machine that will not operate, particularly on an alleged perpetual-motion machine.

Q *What do the terms "patent pending" and "patent applied for" mean?*

A These terms are used by a manufacturer or seller of an article to inform the public that an application for patent on that article is on file in the Patent Office. The law imposes a fine on those who use these terms falsely to deceive the public.

Q *How does one apply for a patent?*

A By making the proper application to the Commissioner of Patents, Washington, D.C. 20231.

Q *Of what does a patent application consist?*

A An application fee, a specification, including claims describing and defining the invention, an oath or declaration, and a drawing if the invention can be illustrated.

Q *What are the Patent Office fees in connection with filing of an application for patent and issuance of the patent?*

A A filing fee of $65 plus certain additional charges for claims depending on their number and the manner of their presentation are required when the application is filed. A final or issue fee of $100 plus certain printing charges are also required if the patent is to be granted. You don't pay this final fee until your application is allowed by the Patent Office.

Q *Are models required as part of the application?*

A Only in the most exceptional cases. The Patent Office has the power to require that a model be furnished, but rarely exercises it.

Q *Can the Patent Office give advice as to whether or not an inventor should apply for a patent?*

A No; the Patent Office can only consider the patentability of an invention when this question comes regularly before it in the form of a patent application.

Q *Is it advisable to conduct a patents search and a search for other records before applying for a patent?*

A Yes; if it is found that the device is shown in some prior patent it is useless to make application. By making a search beforehand, you will save yourself the expense of filing a needless application.

Q *Where can a search be conducted?*

A In the Search Room of the Patent Office at Crystal Plaza, 2021 Jefferson Davis Highway, Arlington, Virginia. Classified and numerically arranged sets of U.S. and foreign patents are kept there for public use.

Q *Will the Patent Office make searches for individuals to help them decide if they should file patent applications?*

A No; but if inventors come to the Patent Office, employees will help them find the proper patent classes in which to make their searches. For a reasonable fee, the Patent Office will furnish lists of patents in any class and subclass, and copies of these patents may be purchased for 50 cents each.

Q *Can I make a patent search or obtain technical information from patents at locations other than the Patent Office Search Room?*

A Yes; some libraries have sets of patent copies numerically arranged in bound volumes, and these patents may be used for search or other information purposes. See the list on pages 74–75.

Q *How can technical information be found in a library collection of patents arranged in bound volumes in numerical order?*

A In a patent library you'll find the **Manual of Classification,** which lists the classes and subclasses that cover the field of your invention or interest. You can then, by referring to microfilm reels or volumes of the **Index of Patents,** identify the patents in these subclasses and look them up. Further information on this subject may be found in the leaflet **Obtaining Information from Patents,** which you can obtain from the Patent Office.

Q *Is it necessary to go to the Patent Office in Washington to transact business concerning patent matters?*

A No; most business with the Patent Office is conducted by correspondence. Interviews regarding pending applications can be arranged with examiners if necessary, however, and are often helpful.

Q *Is there any danger that the Patent Office will give others information contained in my application while it is pending?*

A No; all patent applications are maintained in the strictest secrecy until the patent is issued. After the patent is issued, however, the Patent Office file containing the application and all correspondence leading up to issuance of the patent is made available in the Patent Office Search Room for inspection by anyone, and copies of these files may be purchased from the Patent Office.

Q ***May I write to the Patent Office directly about my application after it is filed?***

A The Patent Office will answer an applicant's inquiries as to the status of the application, and inform him if his application has been rejected, allowed, or is awaiting action by the Patent Office. However, if you have a patent attorney or agent, the Patent Office cannot correspond with both you and the attorney concerning the merits of your application. All comments concerning your invention should be forwarded through your patent attorney or agent.

Q ***What happens when two inventors apply separately for a patent for the same invention?***

A An "interference" is declared and testimony may be submitted to the Patent Office to determine which inventor is entitled to the patent.

Q ***Is there any restriction as to who may obtain a U.S. patent?***

A No; any inventor may obtain a patent regardless of age or sex, by complying with the provisions of the law. A foreign citizen may obtain a patent under exactly the same conditions as a U.S. citizen.

Q ***If two or more people work together to make an invention, to whom will the patent be granted?***

A If several people had a share in the ideas forming the invention, they are joint inventors and a patent will be issued to them jointly on the basis of a proper patent application filed by them jointly. If, on the other hand, one of these people has provided all of the ideas of the invention, and the other has only followed instructions in making it, the person who contributed the ideas is the sole inventor and the patent application and patent will be in his name alone.

Q *If one person furnishes all of the ideas to make an invention and another employs him or furnishes the money for building and testing the invention, should the patent application be filed by them jointly?*

A No; the application must be signed, executed, sworn to, and filed in the Patent Office in the name of the true inventor. This is the person who furnishes the ideas, not the employer or the person who furnishes the money.

Q *May a patent be granted if an inventor dies before filing his application?*

A Yes; the application may be filed by the inventor's executor or administrator.

Q *I have been making and selling my invention for the past 13 months and have not filed a patent application. Is it too late for me to apply for a patent?*

A Yes; you may not obtain a valid patent if the invention was in public use or on sale in this country for more than one year before you filed your patent application. Your own use and sale of the invention will bar your right to a patent just as effectively as though the invention was used and sold by someone else.

Q *I published an article describing my invention in a magazine 13 months ago. Is it too late to apply for a patent?*

A Yes; the fact that you are the author of the article will not save your patent application. The law provides that the inventor is not entitled to a patent if the invention has been described in a printed publication anywhere in the world more than a year before his patent application is filed.

Q *While in England, I found an article that has not been introduced into the United States or patented or described. May I obtain a U.S. patent on this invention?*

A No; only a true inventor may obtain a U.S. patent, not someone who learns of the invention of another.

Q *May the inventor sell or otherwise transfer his right to his patent or patent application to someone else?*

A Yes; he may sell all or any part of his interest in the patent application or patent to anyone by a properly worded assignment. The application must be filed in the Patent Office as the invention of the true inventor, however, and not as the invention of the person who has purchased the invention from him.

Q *If I obtain a patent on my invention, will that protect me against the claims of others who assert that I am infringing on their patents when I make, use, or sell my own invention?*

A No; there may be an unexpired patent of a more basic nature on which your invention is an improvement. If your invention is a detailed refinement or feature of such a basically protected invention, you may not use it without the consent of the patentee, just as no one will have the right to use your patented improvement without your consent during the life of your patent. You should seek competent legal advice before starting to make or sell or use your invention commercially, even though it is protected by a patent granted to you.

Q *Will the Patent Office help me prosecute others if they infringe upon the rights granted to me by my patent?*

A No; the Patent Office has no jurisdiction over questions relating to infringement on patent rights. If your patent is infringed upon, you may sue the infringer in the appropriate U.S. court at your own expense. You may ask for damages for past infringement, royalties for future use, or you may prevent or enjoin the infringer from further use.

Q ***I have made some changes and improvements in my invention since my patent application was filed in the Patent Office. May I amend my patent application by adding a description or illustration of these features?***

A No; the law specifically provides that new matter shall not be introduced into the disclosure of a patent application. However, you should call to the attention of your attorney or agent any such changes you may make or plan to make, so that he may take or recommend any steps that might be necessary for your protection. Perhaps the claims in your application will be sufficiently broad to cover these new features.

Q ***Does a U.S. patent give protection in foreign countries?***

A No; the U.S. patent protects your invention only in this country. If you wish to protect your invention in foreign countries, you must file an application in the Patent Office of each such country within the time permitted by law. This may be quite expensive, because of the cost of filing and prosecuting the individual patent applications and because most foreign countries require payment of taxes to maintain the patents in force. You should ask your practitioner about these costs before you decide to file in foreign countries. In 1978, the European Patent Office opened in Munich. Your patent now protects you

Q ***Does a U.S. patent give protection in foreign countries? (cont.)***

in Belgium, France, West Germany, Great Britain, Luxembourg, the Netherlands, and Switzerland. Also, in 1978 under the Patent Cooperation Treaty, the United States joined with 17 other countries in an international recognition of one another's patents. However, a U.S. International Patent Application is different from the U.S. regular or domestic application.

Q ***Can the Patent Office extend the six-month maximum period for response to an Office action in a pending application?***

A No; this time is fixed by law and the Patent Office cannot extend it. However, the Patent Office can reduce this response time to not less than 30 days. The application will become abandoned unless the Patent Office receives proper response within the time allowed.

Q ***I have not made an invention but have encountered a problem. Can I obtain knowledge through patents of what has been done by others to solve the problem?***

A The patents in the Patent Office Search Room contain a vast wealth of technical information and suggestions, organized in a manner that will enable you to review those most closely related to your field of interest. You may go to Washington and review these patents, or engage a patent practitioner to do this for you and to send you copies of the patents most closely related to your problem.

Q ***How can I be sure that my patent attorney or agent will not reveal the secrets of my invention?***

A Patent attorneys and agents earn their livelihood by the confidential services they perform for their clients.

If an attorney or agent improperly reveals an invention disclosed to him by a client, that attorney or agent is subject to disbarment from further practice before the Patent and Trademark Office and loss of his livelihood. The risk just isn't worth it. Persons who withhold information about their inventions from their attorneys and agents make a serious mistake, for the attorney or agent cannot do a fully effective job unless he is fully informed.

Q ***Are there any organizations that can tell me how and where I may be able to get assistance in developing and marketing my invention?***

A Banks, chambers of commerce, utility companies, and civic-minded organizations interested in industrial growth of the community may be able to help you locate manufacturers and other individuals interested in promoting your ideas. Check your local telephone directory for the district office of the U.S. Department of Commerce or Small Business Administration near you. The Small Business Administration has over 60 offices in various cities and it offers information and counsel to small concerns that are interested in new products. In nearly all states there are planning and development agencies or departments of commerce and industry that seek new product and new process ideas to assist manufacturers and communities in the state. If you do not know the names or addresses of these state organizations, write your governor.

Q ***Are there any organizations that can tell me how and where I may be able to get assistance in developing and marketing my invention?*** **(cont.)**

The Patent and Trademark Office cannot act or advise concerning the business transactions or arrangements that are involved in the development and marketing of an invention. However, it will publish for a $3 service fee a notice in the **Official Gazette** that the patent is available for licensing or sale.

Q ***How do I know if a certain patent-promotion organization is reliable and trustworthy?***

A The Patent and Trademark Office has no control over such organizations and does not supply information about them. Check on the reputation of invention-promotion firms before you make any commitments. Ask the Better Business Bureau in the city where the organization is located if the firm is reliable. On the state level, you can ask the bureau of commerce and industry or consumer affairs. Talk to the banker where the organization does business. Find out from the organization's customers if they are satisfied with the organization's efforts. Check out these organizations in the same way you would choose a new doctor, dentist, lawyer, real esate agent, or tax consultant.

1

Should You Get a Patent?

Let's assume you have the solution to a technical problem and that this solution involves a new and useful process, machine, article of manufacture, or composition of matter. It may be chemical, electrical, or mechanical in nature. Before you learn *how to* get a patent, decide if you *should* get a patent.

Should I? It is important to realize that there is no assurance that you will be granted a patent on your invention. Some people feel that making an invention will automatically make them rich. Not so. Less than 10 percent of the issued patents ever find their way to the marketplace, and even fewer make a profit for the owner. Then again, your invention just might be the one to hit the jackpot. However, even if it is the potential winner, there is a long, hard row to hoe before your patent will show a return on your investment. The point is: Do not spend rent or grocery money on your patent and expect to get your money back soon.

Some inventors get patents knowing full well that they will never get their money back. Why? One reason is the prestige of being an inventor. In the history of the United States, less than five million patents have been granted. Each denotes and recognizes cleverness, originality, and ingenuity on the part of the patentee. If nothing else, the fact that you obtained a patent is persuasive information on a job resumé or a biographical sketch. This alone may justify the effort and expense of getting a patent, especially if you crank one out yourself.

Is it practical? According to law, patent-worthy items must be useful. This criterion *does not* require that your invention is the best, cheapest, and most saleable. It simply requires that the invention serve its purpose. In order to be marketable, it should be practical. To be practical, the invention must be an improvement for which people will be willing to pay. If your invention is added to a machine or article and its cost goes up, will people be willing to pay this extra cost to have your improvement? A few cents extra on some items may make them too expensive to be competitive. On other items, an increase of several dollars may be easily absorbed.

One way to evaluate the worth of your invention is to try to sell it, for cash or on a percentage basis. Suppose, for example, you have invented a new kind of handle for a snow shovel that makes snow shovelling easier, quicker, and less tiring. If conventional snow shovels sell for $5 but with your handle it sells for $7, it may be well worth the extra cost. The sales appeal may create more sales at $7 than the old ones at $5. However, if your new handle runs the cost up so it must sell for $15, the purchaser just may elect to buy the old one at $5. The manufacturer of snow shovels, and his marketing organization, can determine this and make an educated guess as to whether or not your invention is worth the $1,000, $10,000 or $25,000 you are asking.

Most corporations have a form that they ask you to sign before they will look at your idea. You must agree that no confidential relationship exists between you and them, and you must acknowledge the fact that they may have already thought of your invention and that they may already have it under development but not yet out in the marketplace. The form goes on to say that you must rely upon your patent protection should they elect to use your invention. In other words, unless you have or will get a patent, they get your idea for free. If you do have this patent protection (or a patent applied for), then the corporation must and will negotiate with you if they want to use your invention.

A PATENT SEARCH

A patent search will help you determine if your invention is practical when consideration is given to presently known, but not necessarily used, alternate methods of doing the same thing. Not only will you know about the snow shovels sold by your local hardware store, but you'll learn about snow shovels known the world over, many of which have never been made or sold for some reason or another.

A patent search will also help you decide if your invention is really new or if some old patent shows your invention or something similar to it. The search may even unearth something better, in which case you may decide to forget the whole thing. Or, you may decide to license the already patented item and make or market it instead.

Another advantage of a patent search is that you can review the latest patents in your area of interest and use their format in writing your own application. Do not use the format of the old patents because the rules for preparing patent applications have changed through the years.

2

Applying for Your Patent

The patent system is based on the U.S. Constitution, Article 1, for promoting the progress of science and useful arts. During the life of your patent, you have exclusive rights to your invention. You may make and sell it, or you can license it to others for a royalty. This is the patent contract. After your patent has expired, the general public can use your invention without paying you royalties.

The first step in obtaining a patent contract is filing an application. A patent application consists of a *specification*, *drawings*, *declaration*, and *filing fee*. The *specification* includes the *abstract*, *background of the invention*, *summary*, *brief description of the drawings*, *detailed description of the preferred embodiment*, and *claims*. The *declaration*, a printed form on which you fill in the blanks, is attached to the last page of the application.

Before we go into the details of filing an application, here are a few words about the basics. Write simply and clearly. Use small words and short sentences. Organize your thoughts. Get your spouse, an English teacher, or a newspaper reporter to review and criticize what you write. If you can't type well, have a professional typist prepare your application. It should be double-spaced on legal-size paper for easy reading and have ample margins so the examiner can pencil in notes. Number the pages at the bottom, in the center of the page.

For illustrative purposes, I will refer throughout this text to Patent 4,200,324,

United States Patent [19]

Helton

[11] **4,200,324**

[45] **Apr. 29, 1980**

[54] **SHOVEL WITH IMPROVED LIFTING MEANS**

[76] Inventor: **Wayland Helton,** 1351 Nordyke Ave., Indianapolis, Ind. 46221

[21] Appl. No.: **916,140**

[22] Filed: **Jun. 16, 1978**

[51] **Int. Cl.**[2] **A01B 1/22;** B25G 3/38

[52] **U.S. Cl.** **294/58**

[58] **Field of Search** .... 294/54, 57–59; 16/114 R; 37/53; 224/5 B; 403/76, 90; 15/143 R, 144 R, 144 A, 145

[56] **References Cited**

U.S. PATENT DOCUMENTS

617,206	1/1899	Tveit et al.	403/90
2,430,802	11/1947	Catlin	294/58
2,521,441	9/1950	Bickley	294/58
2,826,835	3/1958	O'Shea	294/58 X
3,866,257	2/1975	Cansdale	15/144 R X
4,050,728	9/1977	Davidson	294/58

FOREIGN PATENT DOCUMENTS

1041062	10/1953	France	294/59
1466913	3/1977	United Kingdom	294/58

Primary Examiner—Johnny D. Cherry
Attorney, Agent, or Firm—Woodard, Weikart, Emhardt & Naughton

[57] **ABSTRACT**

A shovel with improved lifting means includes a blade portion, a handle member and a lifting bar. The blade portion has a material-transporting surface and an opposite side rear surface to which one end of the handle is rigidly attached. The lifting bar is attached to the material-transporting surface by a ball and socket connection and extends in length approximately two feet from its point of pivotal attachment. The length of the lifting bar is slightly less than the length of the handle such that the user of the shovel may stand in a substantially upright position and push the shovel forward by means of the handle to collect material on the material-transporting surface, while holding the end of the lifting bar. Once material is collected on the material-transporting surface, the user lifts up on the lifting bar in combination with the handle member in order to move the collected material to another location.

3 Claims, 7 Drawing Figures

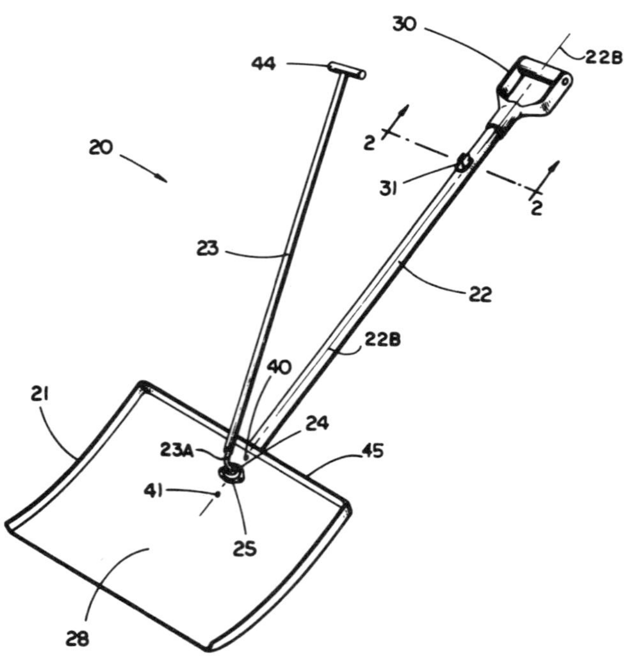

which was issued April 29, 1980, to Wayland Helton for a Shovel with Improved Lifting Means. The first page of the patent is reproduced on page 20 for reference.

THE SPECIFICATION

In the specification, describe your invention as precisely as possible. Begin with the title of your invention, then set forth the abstract, background of the invention, summary, brief description of the drawings, detailed description of the preferred embodiment, and claims.

The Abstract

The abstract is a very short paragraph that describes the invention. On the final patent, it will appear on the first page and a drawing of your invention will appear below it. Together, the abstract and drawing enable a searcher to decide quickly if your invention is of further interest to him. Companies pay searchers to look for new products. If your abstract and front-page drawing appeal to a searcher, you might have a buyer for your invention. For the front page, the examiner picks the view in your drawings that best illustrates your invention. You have no control over which one will be used. You do write your own abstract, however.

Read the Helton abstract. It tells you exactly what the invention is and what it does. It is a shovel with a lifting bar attached to the material-transporting surface by a ball-and-socket connection. The user lifts up on the lifting bar in combination with the handle member for easier movement of the collected material from one location to another.

Background of the Invention

Here is your chance to brag about your invention. Convince the examiner that there really is a problem to be solved and that you are not just presenting another way of accomplishing the same old thing. If you don't, the examiner is likely to reject your invention as being of interest only to someone skilled in the art.

Identify the problems in devices that are already in existence and list the advantages your invention has over them. State the general area of your invention. Helton says his invention relates to shovels with auxiliary lifting aids. He then explains the hardships involved in using ordinary snow shovels: how they tire the user, strain the lower back, strain the wrist when the user tries to balance the load, and aggravate preexisting injuries. He then tells how people have improved upon the conventional snow shovel, and how they fail or do it differently than he does with his invention.

This invention relates in general to shovels and in particular to shovels with auxiliary lifting aids.

Shovels, such as for example, snow shovels, are a combination of a blade and handle arranged so that to effectively use the shovel, the handle must be grasped at two spaced apart locations and the user must bend over to such degree that the user's upper body is almost horizontal with respect to the ground. This particular user position results in significant strain to the lower back area and in addition to more rapidly tiring the user, this strain, may accelerate back injuries or aggravate preexisting injuries. A further disadvantage of such conventional snow shovel designs is that the handle is round and the blade is wide and extends for several inches on either side of the handle, and when material is loaded onto the blade, balancing of the load becomes quite difficult. A still further disadvantage is that the hand of the user which is positioned closest to the blade is twisted when the load on the blade is to be dumped and this twisting places a severe strain on the wrist. In an effort to overcome certain shortcomings and to improve aspects of snow shovel designs, the following list

of patents disclose design features which have been conceived.

Patent No.	Patentee	Issue Date
61,784	Wheat	2/05/67
389,092	Mercer	9/04/88
3,751,094	Bohler	8/07/73
606,534	Gifford	6/28/98
930,660	Gifford	8/10/09
2,967,363	Meier	1/10/61
781,772	Gifford	2/07/05

Wheat discloses a snow shovel design wherein a short secondary or auxiliary handle is locked to the body of the shovel by means of the ordinary handle. The short auxiliary handle includes an opening for easy grasping and is rigidly attached adjacent one end of the blade, but is not attached directly to the blade.

Mercer discloses a snow scraper which may also serve as a snow shovel and a secondary grip means is provided along the back edge of the blade portion in addition to the cross bar member which serves as the primary means for pushing the snow scraper device.

Bohler discloses an auxiliary handle which is readily securable to a regular handle of an implement such as a shovel, rake or hoe and is designed to be grasped by a person's one hand while the person's other hand grasps the regular handle.

Gifford U.S. Pat. No. 606,534 discloses a snow shovel design which includes an auxiliary hand-grip attached to the regular handle at a location which is spaced apart from the rear edge of the shovel blade portion.

Gifford U.S. Pat. No. 930,660 discloses a snow shovel which includes an adjustable lift handle attached to the main handle portion of the shovel. This particular handle member is similar in design and location to the handle member of the previously listed Gifford U.S. Pat. No. 606,534 and as such, is positioned close to the rear edge of the blade portion of the shovel and extends in length for only a few inches. Thus, the user of such a shovel, as well as the previous Gifford designed shovel, must bend forward and over the shovel in order to grip both the auxiliary handle as well as the primary handle.

Gifford U.S. Pat. No. 781,772 discloses a snow shovel similar in design and construction to the previously two listed Gifford patents and includes a similarly styled auxiliary handle. Although there may be patentable differences between the three Gifford patents, the features which are relevant to the present invention are the size, location and construction of the auxiliary handle, and the designs disclosed do not overcome the disadvantage of having to bend at the waist to almost a horizontal position with respect to the ground in order to utilize the particular shovels.

Meier discloses a manually operated snow plow which includes a handle bar attached to the blade in such a manner that the blade may be adjusted to various angular positions with respect to the handle bar.

While some of the above-listed patents provide gripping means at a second, or auxiliary gripping location space apart from the free end of the primary handle, none of the above patents provide means by which the disadvantage of requiring the user to bend sharply at his waist may be overcome and thus, it would be an improvement to these designs if such means could be provided. Furthermore, none of the above-listed patents disclose an auxiliary handle which attaches directly to the material-transporting surface of the blade portion which reduces the moment arm between the weight and the point of lifting force and makes the load seem lighter.

Summary of the Invention

In the background, you discussed the problems to be solved and the defects or disadvantages of the previous inventions. In the summary, describe how you solve these problems with your invention. Logically convince the examiner that you really do have an invention worthy of patent protection. A good summary will also convince a manufacturer that your invention is a marketable improvement.

Helton's summary could be more effective. It says that his shovel has a handle secured to the blade portion and that the means for lifting the blade portion is attached directly to the blade portion. That's not enough. In the background, he mentioned the failures of earlier patents. In the summary, he should tell how he overcomes these failures.

A shovel according to one embodiment of the present invention comprises a blade portion having a handle secured to the blade portion and means for lifting the blade portion attached directly to the blade portion.

One object of the present invention is to provide an

improved shovel of the type having auxiliary lifting means.

Related objects and advantages of the present invention will be apparent from the following description.

Brief Description of the Drawings

In this section, you simply state what your drawings illustrate: FIG. 1 is a perspective view, FIG. 2 is a sectional view taken along line 2-2 in FIG. 1, FIG. 3 is a partial side view, and so on. FIG. 1 shows what? A shovel with auxiliary lifting means. FIG. 2 shows the retaining clip. FIG. 3 shows the ball-and-socket connection. Helton has chosen views that best illustrate his invention and describes briefly just what these views are and what they show. Read Helton's description and plan your own accordingly.

FIG. 1 is a perspective view of a shovel with auxiliary lifting means according to a typical embodiment of the present invention.

FIG. 2 is a section view of a retaining clip comprising a portion of the FIG. 1 shovel and taken along line 2—2 in FIG. 1.

FIG. 3 is a partial side view of the FIG. 1 shovel detailing a ball and socket connection which comprises a portion of the FIG. 1 shovel.

FIG. 4 is a side elevation view of the FIG. 1 shovel illustrating movement of an auxiliary handle which comprises a portion of the FIG. 1 shovel.

FIG. 5 is a perspective view of an alternate form of a shovel according to a typical embodiment of the present invention.

FIG. 6 is a partial perspective view of the handle of the FIG. 5 shovel.

FIG. 7 is a partial side elevation view similar to FIG. 4 of an alternative embodiment of the present invention.

Description of the Preferred Embodiment

Now comes the difficult job of describing the "nuts and bolts" of the invention. In the description you describe the parts, how they fit together, and how they cooperate to perform the function intended. Unless dimensions are critical, you may omit them.

There are several ways to approach description writing. You can assume the readers do not have access to the drawings and write so precisely that they could sketch the invention from your description. Or, you can assume that the drawings are in front of them and that the description merely aids in understanding the drawings. Obviously, it is much harder to write the first type of description. You can also write somewhere in between by describing in great detail the inventive details and more briefly the areas that are obvious and well known.

For the purposes of promoting an understanding of the principles of the invention, reference will now be made to the embodiment illustrated in the drawings and specific language will be used to describe the same. It will nevertheless be understood that no limitation of the scope of the invention is thereby intended, such alterations and further modifications in the illustrated device, and such further applications of the principles of the invention as illustrated therein being contemplated as would normally occur to one skilled in the art to which the invention relates.

Referring to FIG. 1, there is illustrated a shovel 20 which is similar in size, shape and general configuration to a snow shovel. Shovel 20 includes a blade portion 21, a primary handle member 22, auxiliary lifting means in the form of rigid bar 23 and a ball 24 and socket 25 connection joining one end of rigid bar 23 to blade portion 21. Blade portion 21 includes a front edge, a rear upturned edge and two upturned side edges. Socket 25 is rigidly secured to the material-transferring outer surface 28 of blade portion 21 at a location coincident with the longitudinal axis 22B of handle 22 and adjacent the rear edge of the blade portion by a suitable metal-to-metal joining technique such as, for example,

welding. One end of handle member **22** is rigidly attached to the opposite, rear surface **29** of blade portion **21** and includes a free end hand grip **30** which is typically grasped by one hand of the user of the shovel. Securely attached to handle member **22** at a location which is adjacent hand grip **30** is a bar-retaining clip **31** (see FIG. 2) which is fastened to handle member **22** by means of two fasteners **32**. The open region **33** of retaining clip **31** is suitably sized widthwise and depthwise to receive rigid bar **23**. Clip tabs **36** and **37** are constructed of a material which has certain spring properties to it and are positioned relative to each other such that they must be slightly forced apart as bar **23** is pushed into open region **33**.

Handle member **22** is attached to the rear surface **29** of blade portion **21** by means of retaining brackets **38** and **39**, and although brackets **38** and **39** may be all that comprises the attaching means, it is preferred to also incorporate threaded fasteners **40** and **41** extending through blade portion **21** into handle member **22** (see FIG. 3). A single sleeve may be used in lieu of brackets **38** and **39**, such that handle member **22** would slide into the sleeve and be secured by fasteners. The ball and socket connection of bar **23** to surface **28** enables bar **23** to be moved a maximum of 180 degrees in any direction such that the cumulative result of the motion of bar **23** would be the sweeping out of a hemispherical shape. Bar **23** is joined to ball **24** by means of a generally L-shaped neck member **23A** which is of a reduced lateral cross-sectional area with respect to bar **23**. Member **23A** is formed into two portions wherein when bar **23** is in a folded position against handle **22**, one portion is substantially perpendicular to the longitudinal axis **22B** and the other portion is substantially parallel to axis **22B**. However, due to the particular application for shovel **20**, primary movement of bar **23** will be between a folded position parallel to handle member **20** and an extended position (see FIG. 4) wherein bar **23** pivots away from handle member **22** and defines an acute included angle with handle member **22**. Secondary movement will be in a left or right pivoting direction from the extended position, such as required to dump material off of surface **28**.

In normal operation, such as when shoveling snow, one hand of the user will grasp hand grip **30** and the other hand of the user will grasp T-shaped cross bar **44** at the free end of bar **23**. When snow is being removed from a sidewalk or driveway or similar surface, the hands of the user will typically be in line with one another and substantially parallel with the axis of handle member 22. In this particular mode, a basic hinge arrangement would be suitable to connect rigid bar **23** to surface **28**. However, once surface **28** is loaded with collected material, such as snow, the material must be removed to a remote location and dumped so that surface **28** can be emptied and returned to a ready condition in order to pick up additional material. When such dumping is to occur, a basic hinge arrangement would require that both hands of the user turn with the shovel and this puts a twist in and strain on the wrist of the hand grasping cross bar **44**. Consequently, the inclusion of a ball **24** and socket **25** connection permits the hand grasping cross bar **44** to remain in a palm-down orientation while the other hand which is grasping hand grip **30** performs the twisting and dumping thereby allowing the ball and socket location to be the pivoting point for such twisting-dumping motion.

Rigid bar **23** is approximately **26** inches in length from its ball and socket point of attachment to cross bar **44** and is slightly shorter than the length of handle member **22** from blade portion edge **45** to hand grip **30**. This 26-inch length is based on a handle design which is approximately 29 inches in length and thus, it is preferred that the length of rigid bar **23** be at least 80% of the length of handle member **22**. This enables the user of shovel **20** to stand in a substantially upright position with one arm extended downwardly and with the hand of the downwardly extending arm grasping hand grip **30** while the opposite arm extends outwardly in the direction that the shovel is moving and grasps cross bar **44**. This user position relieves the strain on the lower back as well as reduces shoulder and upper arm exertion in that the ball and socket connection and the presence of bar **23** enables snow to be removed with primarily only lifting and wrist pivoting actions and without bending at the waist.

Referring to FIG. 5, shovel **47** illustrates an alternate form wherein rigid bar **23** is replaced by a length of flexible material, such as rope **48**. One end of rope **48** is attached to eye bolt **49** which may be either bolted to surface **50** or the head portion of eye bolt **49** may be welded to surface **50**. The retaining clip which was previously positioned on the handle member has been replaced by a clearance hole **51** similarly disposed at the free end adjacent to the handle grip. The free end of rope **48** includes a wooden cross member **52** through which rope **48** passes. Cross member **52** provides a convenient gripping means for the hand of the user and when rope **48** is not being used as an auxiliary lifting means, cross member **52** may be inserted into clearance hole **51** (see FIG. 6) as a means of storage and retention. Rope **48** has an overall length similar to that of bar **23** such that the user orientation of a substantially upright position when using shovel **20** would be equally applicable with either rigid bar **23** or with rope **48**. It is also possible to provide both rigid bar **23** and rope **48** as part of the same device such that either auxiliary means

could be used and one could be employed as a backup. Referring to FIG. 4, it can be seen that the hand grip 30 is arranged in the illustrated preferred embodiment as aligned with the shank portion 22A of the handle member 22. This is the preferred arrangement of the shovel. However, the shovel can also be constructed with the hand grip 30A at approximately 45 degrees to the shank portion 22A as shown in FIG. 7 as well as at other angles.

It is to be understood that although a snow shovel has been illustrated, the various features of the disclosed invention are equally well suited to virtually every type of shovel design and although various materials and connection techniques are possible, the optimum materials and dimensions will depend in part on the basic shovel style and size as well as its intended application.

While the invention has been illustrated and described in detail in the drawings and foregoing description, the same is to be considered as illustrative and not restrictive in character, it being understood that only the preferred embodiment has been shown and described and that all changes and modifications that come within the spirit of the invention are desired to be protected.

Claims

Volumes have been written on claim drafting. This discussion won't make you an expert, but it will show you how to write claims suitable for filing. Don't be afraid to ask the examiner to suggest wording for your claims as the prosecution of your application proceeds. Examiners are usually very helpful, especially when the inventor is handling his own application.

The claims define your invention. Its patentability will be based on your claims. If the examiner allows one or more of your claims, you'll get your patent.

Before you write the claims, make a list of the essential elements. For the Helton invention, these would be "shovel with blade and handle," "auxiliary lifting means," and "means to attach." Under "auxiliary lifting means," you could add other limitations, such as "rigid bar," "rope with handle," "means to store." Under "means to attach," you could add "ball-and-socket connection," "details," "pivot connection," and "eye bolt." Your scratch pad would look like this:

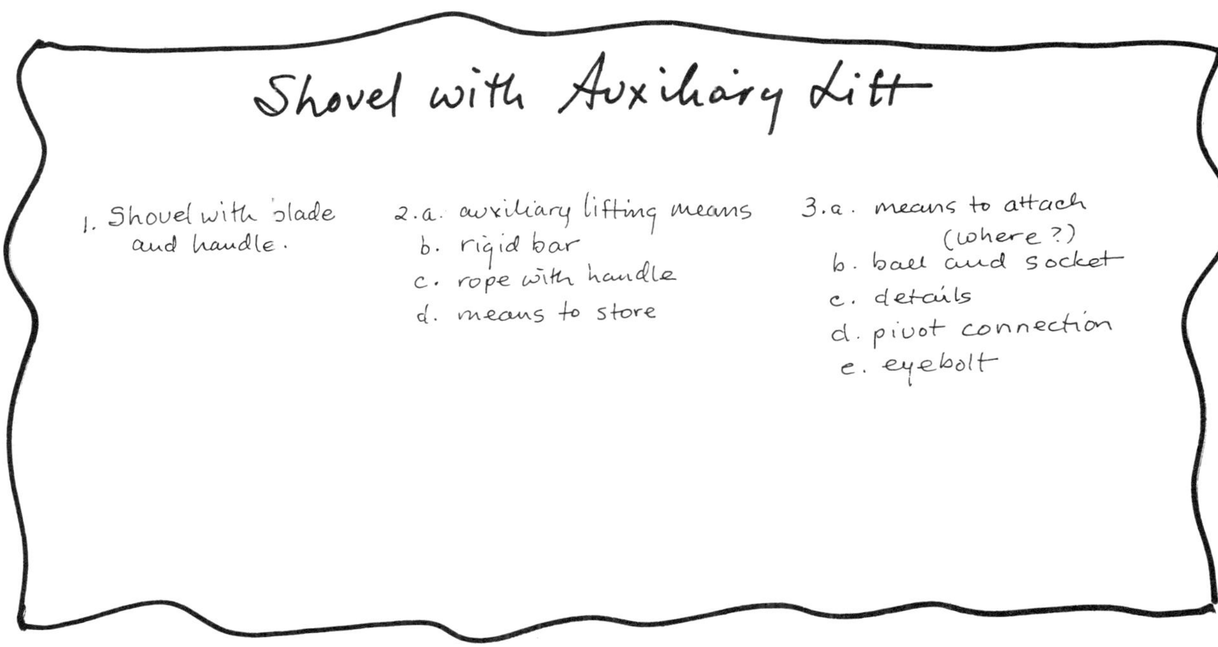

The first claim should be as broad as possible. Referring back to the scratch pad, you would include a shovel with blade and handle, an auxiliary lifting means, and the means to attach the auxiliary lifting means to the blade of the shovel. Notice that structure, as opposed to function, is being claimed. Functional language, such as "whereby a load may be lifted and moved more easily," serves as a constant reminder of what the invention accomplishes. The first claim for the Helton snow shovel would read:

1. In combination,
a shovel having a blade portion with a handle attached thereto,
an auxiliary lifting means,
said lifting means being attached to said shovel near said blade portion, whereby a load may be more easily lifted and moved.

This is broader than the claim that appears on the final patent. The reason is this: It is too broad, and was limited during the prosecution of the patent application. We will see how claims are limited as we follow the patent application through the entire process.

For the basic filing fee of $65, you are permitted one independent claim and up to nine dependent claims. Claims 2 and 3 of the Helton patent are dependent claims. Notice how the claims become more restrictive. Claim 2 imposes the further requirement that one of the neck-member portions in Claim 1 is perpendicular to the handle axis and the other portion is parallel to it. Claim 3 says that in addition to what's stated in Claims 1 and 2, the rigid bar must be of a certain length relative to the length of the handle. Referring back to the scratch pad, you can see that other claims could include a rigid bar and ball and socket, a rope with handle and an eye bolt, and a rigid bar with a pivot connection. Still another dependent claim could include the means to store, such as the hole and clip mechanism. Look at the claims on the final patent to see how they incorporate these elements.

What is claimed is:
1. In combination:
a shovel having a blade portion and a handle secured to said blade portion;
auxiliary lifting means connected to said blade portion and cooperatively arranged with said handle for lifting said blade portion, said blade portion including an outer surface and an oppositely disposed rear surface, said handle being secured to said rear surface;
means for attaching said auxiliary lifting means to said outer surface, said attaching means including a ball member and a socket member arranged into a ball and socket connection;
said auxiliary lifting means including a rigid bar having gripping means at one end and a neck member extending from the opposite end, said neck member joining said opposite end to the ball member of said ball and socket connection; and
said neck portion is substantially L-shaped into two portions and is of a reduced lateral cross-sectional area compared to said rigid bar.

2. The combination of claim 1 wherein when said rigid bar is in a folded position against said handle, one of said neck member portions is disposed substantially perpendicular to the longitudinal axis of said handle and the other portion is disposed substantially parallel to said axis.

3. The combination of claim 2 wherein said rigid bar extends in length a distance equal to at least 80 percent of the overall length of said handle.

DRAWINGS

Everything in your claims (see pages 25–26) must be shown in your drawings, which show your invention in perspective. Various views will show different details of your invention. Identify the different drawings as FIG. 1, FIG. 2, and so on. "FIG." must be capitalized and punctuated. Each part of your invention is numbered in the drawings, and a part retains the same number in the various views. That is, the material-transporting surface in the Helton drawings will be identified as part 28 in all the views. Draw lead lines between the parts and the identifying numbers. The numerals should be ⅛-inch high so that in printing they can be reduced to $\frac{1}{24}$-inch high.

Plan what drawings you need to illustrate your invention best. Remember, all elements in the claims must be shown in the drawings. Look at the Helton drawings on pages 27–29. FIG. 1 is a perspective view of the shovel with auxiliary lifting means. It is a good overall view of the invention. The other

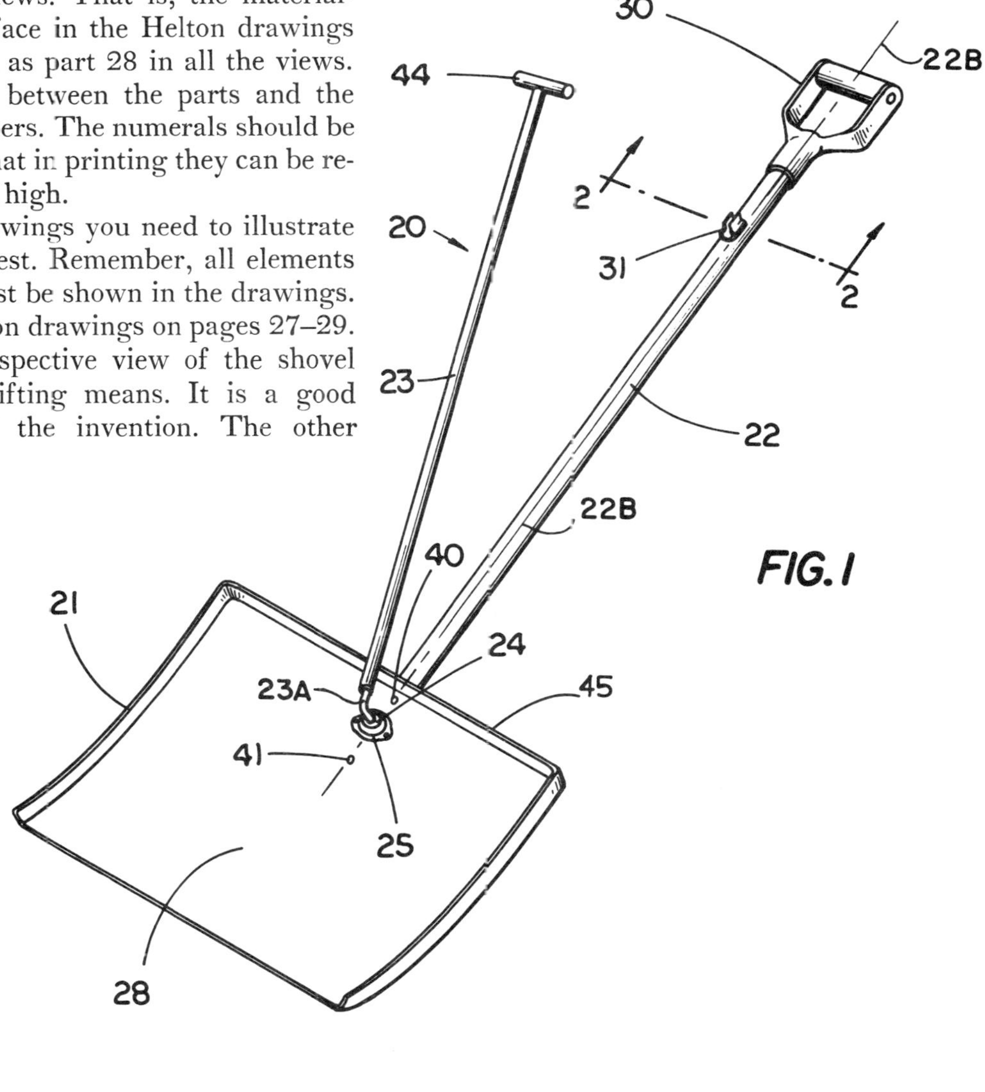

FIG. 1

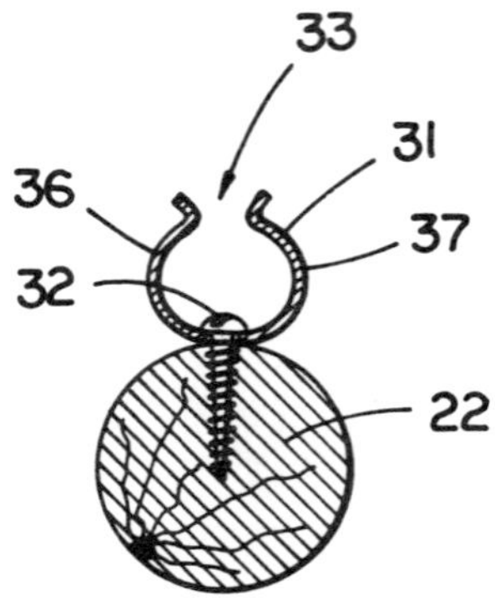

FIG. 2

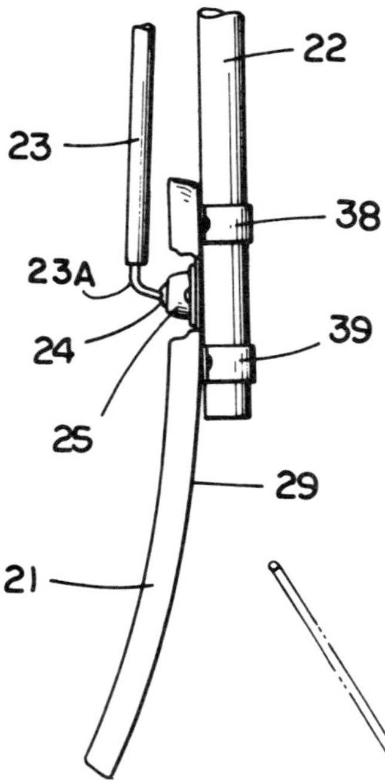

FIG. 3

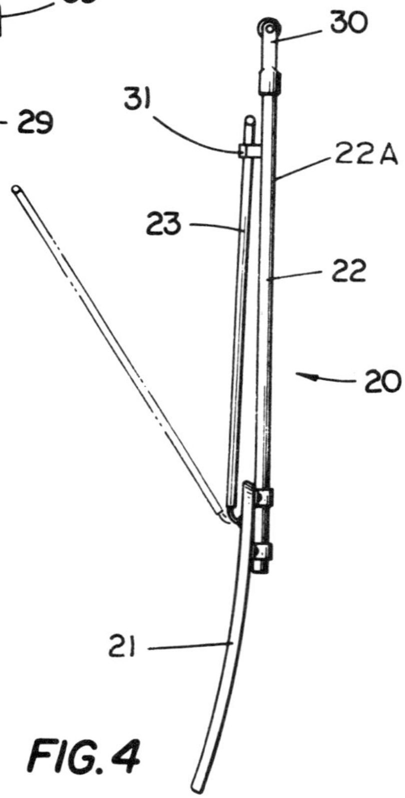

FIG. 4

drawings show more detailed views of the invention. FIG. 2 shows a sectional view. FIG. 3 is a side view showing how the ball and socket connects to the shovel. FIG. 4 shows how the auxiliary handle moves and fastens to the clip (31) for storage. FIG. 5 shows perspective views of an eye bolt (49), rope (48), handle (52), and clearance hole (51). The handle (52) and the clearance hole (51) are shown in even greater detail in FIG. 6. FIG. 7 is a side view showing how the handle (30A) is tilted relative to the shank portion (22A).

Draw on pure white paper of a thickness corresponding to two-ply or three-ply bristol board. The paper should permit you to erase and make corrections. You must use India ink to secure perfectly solid black lines for clear reproduction. You must erase mistakes; you may not cover them with white pigment. The drawing sheet must be 8½-inches wide and 14-inches long. The top margin must be 2 inches and the side and bottom margins must be ¼ inch each. This leaves a drawing area of 8 inches by 11¾ inches. All work must be confined in the drawing area. You may not use margin border lines.

Make hatch marks in sectional views with oblique parallel lines not less than 1/20 inch apart. Use shading, assuming that the light is coming from the upper left-hand corner at a 45-degree angle. Make your drawings to a large enough scale so the views are not crowded when they are reduced to two-thirds of the original size in reproduction. Mail your drawings flat, protected from creasing and bending, or in a mailing tube. Never fold them.

If your drawings do not comply strictly to the rules, you may ask a Patent Office draftsman to correct them. In the first Office action (see page 33), the examiner will state his objections to the drawings. Using his language, ask the draftsman to make the corrections. You will be charged a nominal fee for this work.

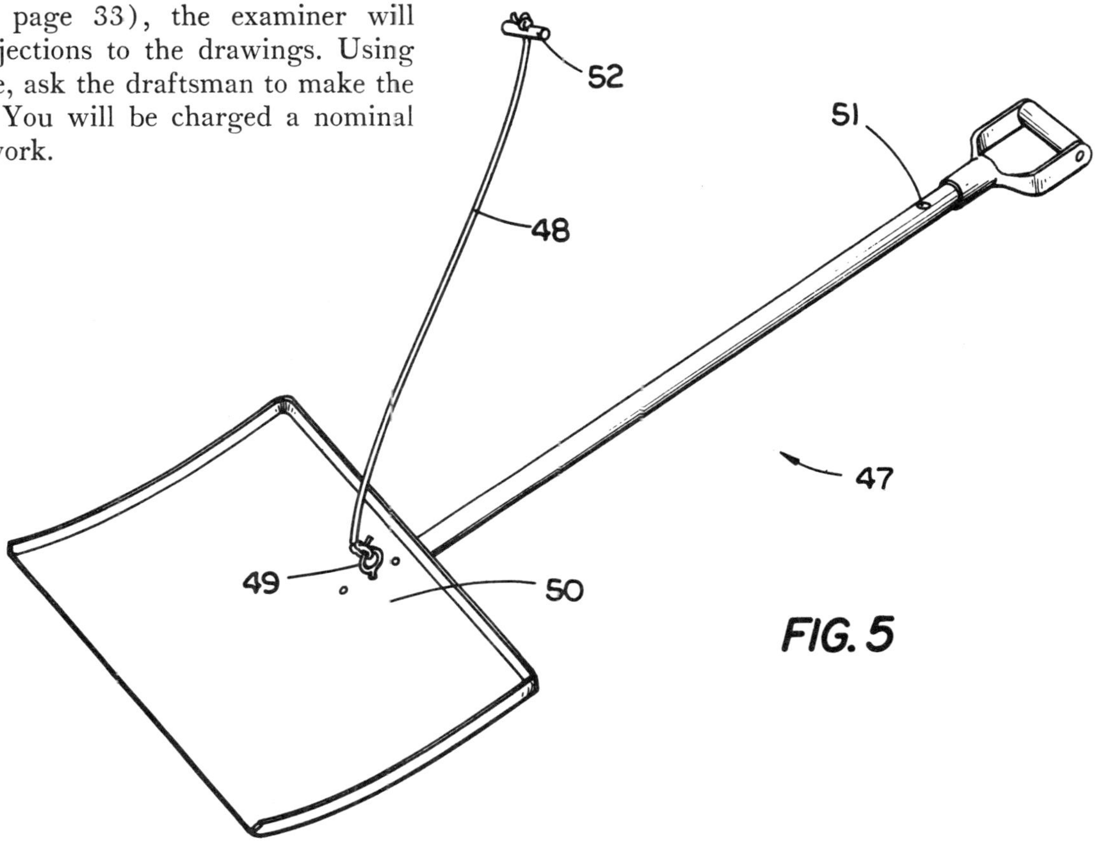

FIG. 5

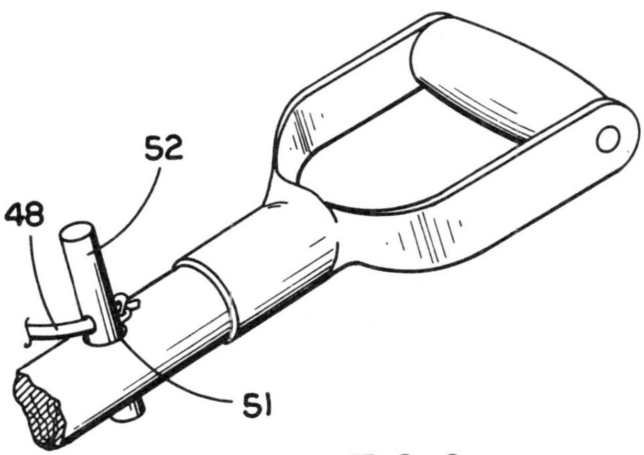

FIG. 6

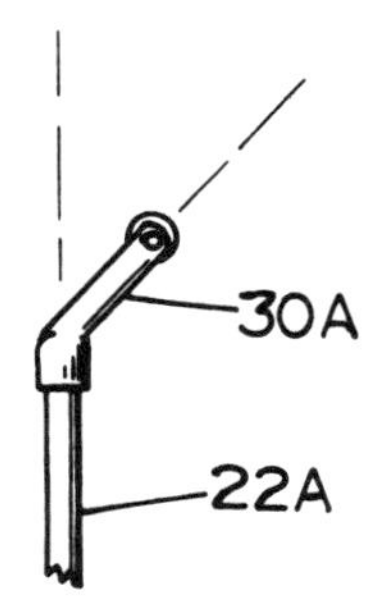

FIG. 7

COMBINED DECLARATION AND POWER OF ATTORNEY IN ORIGINAL APPLICATION	ATTORNEY DOCKET NO.

As a below named inventor, I hereby declare that:

my residence, post office address and citizenship are as stated below next to my name; that

I verily believe that I am the original, first and sole inventor (if only one name is listed below) or a joint inventor (if plural inventors are named below) of the invention entitled: ______________________

____

described and claimed in the attached specification, that I understand the content of the attached specification, that I do not know and do not believe the same was ever known or used in the United States of America before my or our invention thereof, or patented or described in any printed publication in any country before my or our invention thereof or more than one year prior to this application, that the same was not in public use or on sale in the United States of America more than one year prior to this application, that the invention has not been patented or made the subject of an inventor's certificate issued before the date of this application in any country foreign to the United States of America on an application filed by me or my legal representatives or assigns more than twelve months prior to this application, that I acknowledge my duty to disclose information of which I am aware which is material to the examination of this application, and that no application for patent or inventor's certificate on this invention has been filed in any country foreign to the United States of America prior to this application by me or my legal representatives or assigns, except as follows: ______________________

______________________.

I hereby appoint the following attorney(s) and/or agent(s) to prosecute this application and to transact all business in the Patent and Trademark Office connected therewith: ______________________

______________________.

Address all telephone calls to ______________________ at telephone no. ____________.

Address all correspondence to ______________________.

I hereby declare that all statements made herein of my own knowledge are true and that all statements made on information and belief are believed to be true; and further that these statements were made with the knowledge that willful false statements and the like so made are punishable by fine or imprisonment, or both, under Section 1001 of Title 18 of the United States Code and that such willful false statements may jeopardize the validity of the application or any patent issued thereon.

FULL NAME OF SOLE OR FIRST INVENTOR	INVENTOR'S SIGNATURE	DATE
RESIDENCE		CITIZENSHIP
POST OFFICE ADDRESS		

FULL NAME OF SECOND JOINT INVENTOR, IF ANY	INVENTOR'S SIGNATURE	DATE
RESIDENCE		CITIZENSHIP
POST OFFICE ADDRESS		

FULL NAME OF THIRD JOINT INVENTOR, IF ANY	INVENTOR'S SIGNATURE	DATE
RESIDENCE		CITIZENSHIP
POST OFFICE ADDRESS		

DECLARATION

The declaration is a printed form, PTO-258 (10-77), which must be filled in and included as the last page of the application, right after the claims. A declaration form is reprinted on page 30; read it carefully.

FILING FEE

You must include a filing fee with your application. This fee is based on the number of claims you submit. The minimum is $65, which includes one independent claim and up to nine dependent claims. Each additional independent claim costs $10 and each additional dependent claim costs $2.

FILING THE APPLICATION

Before you seal the envelope, make a last-minute check. The application consists of: the specification, which includes the abstract, background, summary, brief description of the drawings, description of the preferred embodiment, and claims, drawings, declaration form, and the filing fee. Keep an exact copy of everything you file. During the prosecution of your application, the examiner will says things like, "Lead line 21 in FIG. 2 points to the wrong element. Correction is required." If you don't keep a file, you won't be able to respond to his comments.

The Patent Office recommends, although it does not insist upon, three more pieces of paper: a brief note that states how many independent claims and dependent claims there are in your application and therefore how big your filing fee is (remember, your filing fee varies with the number of claims you submit); a list of the existing patents closest to your invention with an explanation as to how your patent differs from each; and a self-addressed and stamped postcard, on which the Patent Office will put the date it received your application and the serial number it assigns. The Office will mail the postcard back to you. This way, you'll have proof that you complied with the date requirements.

When all is ready, mail your application to the Commissioner of Patents, Washington, D.C. 20231. Be sure to affix the correct postage. If not, your application will be returned to you, delaying the filing date—an important issue in the event of an interference, a proceeding to determine which of two inventors of the same invention gets the patent (see page 48).

Once the Patent Office has received your application, you may mark your product with "Pat. Pend.," "Patent Pending," or "Patent Applied For." It's against the law to use these terms unless you actually do have an application pending or on file in the Patent Office.

It takes about a year for the Patent Office to respond to your application. Use this time to sell your invention to a manufacturer. However, a word of caution: Do not let the potential buyer see the claims, declaration, serial number, or filing date. An unscrupulous manufacturer with this knowledge may try to file an application and concoct evidence of prior inventorship to win an interference proceeding against you.

Application Checklist

- Type, double-spaced, on legal-size paper.
- Write simply and clearly. Organize your thoughts and use short sentences and simple words.
- Make sure your claims define your invention. Remember, it is the claims that will determine the patentability of the invention.
- Include everything in your claims in your drawings. Draw with India ink on pure-white paper corresponding to two-ply or three-ply bristol board. The drawing sheet must be 8½-inches wide and 14-inches long.
- Include the filing fee (the minimum is $65) with your application.
- Keep an exact copy of everything you file.
- Include a self-addressed, stamped envelope to verify receipt of your application.

3

The Office Action

The Patent Office will respond to your application with several forms. The first one is PTOL-326. A sample copy is shown on page 35. Read it carefully. Notice the stamp that says "Mailed" and gives the date and group number. The date is extremely important. It establishes an absolute deadline for your response to the Office action. The maximum time limit is six months, although the examiner has the power to set a shorter response time. On the sample form, notice that the examiner has shortened the response time to three months.

In Part I, the examiner indicates what he is enclosing. Part II is a Summary of Action. By checking certain of the 11 boxes, the examiner lets you know in a hurry what action he has taken. Box 3 indicates what claims have been allowed, box 4 tells what claims have been rejected, and box 5 tells what claims are objected to. If box 10 is marked, celebrate. It means that except for formal matters, the application is allowable and all claims remaining in the application have been granted. In other words, you've gotten your patent. However, this seldom happens on the examiner's first Office action.

The next part of the Office action is the Notification of Rejections and/or Objections, which is drawn up on Form PTO-1142. A sample copy is shown on page 36. The notification tells an applicant why a claim was rejected or objected to. The applicant then has the chance to amend the claims or to justify them in light of the examiner's comments.

Look at the sample notification. Claims 1 through 6 are rejected on the grounds of 35 U.S.C. 103. As the note at the bottom of the page says, Sections 100, 101, 102, 103, and 112 of the Patent Statute (Title 35 of the U.S. Code) are printed on the reverse side. They are shown here on page 38. U.S.C. 103 says a patent cannot be granted if an invention closely resembles and performs the same function as existing devices. In the References column, the examiner has cited A/B. These letters refer to patents that are listed on yet another form, PTO-892. A sample is shown on page 37. As you can see, "A" means Voehl and "B" refers to Frankel, et al. So, what is the examiner telling you? Claims 1 through 6 are unpatentable because they relate to obvious subject matter in view of Voehl or Frankel. In other words, your invention resembles Voehl's and Frankel's to such a degree that a patent cannot be granted.

Claim 7 is objected to because it is dependent on a rejected claim. If you rewrite it as an independent claim, the examiner might allow it. Claim 8 is unpatentable under 35 U.S.C. 102 in view of Glahe. U.S.C. 102 says an invention cannot be patented if it duplicates—as opposed to resembles—an already existing invention. So, claim 8 is rejected because it duplicates Glahe.

For your convenience, copies of the patents listed on Form PTO-892 are enclosed with the Office action. Look them over and review the entire Office action. Set it aside for a few days and let it rest. Look it over again. If you still do not understand it, call the examiner and ask him to go over it with you and explain it. You'll find his name and telephone number at the bottom of Form PTO-1142. Don't argue with him or try to convince him he was wrong. Whether or not you agree with him, try to understand why he is rejecting your application. Once you understand his reasoning, you can frame your arguments and modify your claims so he will accept them.

Don't be discouraged by the examiner's negative attitude. His criticism actually pinpoints the patentable features of your invention and smokes out your arguments. A negative Office action is not necessarily fatal. If you can effectively argue with the examiner and make the necessary changes in your claims, he'll take you seriously and help you get your patent.

The examiner's thorough patent search is very important. If your patent is ever contested on the grounds that the examiner failed to consider a prior patent when he granted your claims, a court could invalidate his action. For that matter, if the examiner fails to mention a prior patent that you think can have a bearing on your invention, you must bring it to his attention. You agreed to do this when you signed the declaration.

UNITED STATES DEPARTMENT OF COMMERCE
Patent and Trademark Office
Address: COMMISSIONER OF PATENTS AND TRADEMARKS
Washington, D.C. 20231

SERIAL NUMBER	FILING DATE	FIRST NAMED APPLICANT	ATTORNEY DOCKET NO.
044,836	06/01/79		

EXAMINER	
H. H. Hunter	
ART UNIT	PAPER NUMBER
353	2

MAILED
MAY 6 1980
GROUP 350

This is a communication from the examiner in charge of your application.
COMMISSIONER OF PATENTS AND TRADEMARKS

☒ This application has been examined. ☐ Responsive to communication filed on ________ ☐ This action is made final.

A shortened statutory period for response to this action is set to expire 3 month(s), ________ days from the date of this letter.
Failure to respond within the period for response will cause the application to become abandoned. 35 U.S.C. 133

Part I THE FOLLOWING ATTACHMENT(S) ARE PART OF THIS ACTION:

1. ☒ Notice of References Cited, Form PTO-892.
2. ☐ Notice of Informal Patent Drawing, PTO-948.
3. ☐ Notice of Informal Patent Application, Form PTO-152.
4. ☐ ________

Part II SUMMARY OF ACTION

1. ☒ Claims 1 – 8 are pending in the application.

   Of the above, claims ________ are withdrawn from consideration.
2. ☐ Claims ________ have been cancelled.
3. ☐ Claims ________ are allowed.
4. ☒ Claims 1 – 6, 8 are rejected.
5. ☒ Claims 7 are objected to.
6. ☐ Claims ________ are subject to restriction or election requirement.
7. ☐ The formal drawings filed on ________ are acceptable.
8. ☐ The drawing correction request filed on ________ has been ☐ approved. ☐ disapproved.
9. ☐ Acknowledgment is made of the claim for priority under 35 U.S.C. 119. The certified copy has ☐ been received. ☐ not been received. ☐ been filed in parent application, serial no. ________ filed on ________
10. ☐ Since this application appears to be in condition for allowance except for formal matters, prosecution as to the merits is closed in accordance with the practice under Ex parte Quayle, 1935 C.D. 11; 453 O.G. 213.
11. ☐ Other

PTOL-326 (rev. 10-78)

EXAMINER'S FIRST ACTION

FORM PTO-1142 (3-75)

U.S. DEPARTMENT OF COMMERCE
Patent and Trademark Office

PART III

SERIAL NUMBER 044 436

GROUP ART UNIT 353

NOTIFICATION OF REJECTION(S) AND/OR OBJECTION(S) (35 USC 132)

	CLAIMS (1)	REASONS FOR REJECTION (2)	REFERENCES * (3)	INFORMATION IDENTIFICATION AND COMMENTS (4)
1	1-6	35UC 103	A/B	The claims are generally readable on both A and B, any distinction thereover being essentially matters of choice and/or expediency.
2	7			Objected to as a dependent claim depending upon a rejected claim. When rewritten in independent form, it's allowance will be considered.
3	8	USC 102	G	All elements of claim 8 are found in G
4				
5	C, D, E, F and G all show additional features as claimed and should be carefully considered as potential basic references in light of any amendments.			

EXAMINER H. Hunter

TEL. NO. (703) -557 - 3414

* Capital letters representing references are identified on accompanying Form PTO-892.
The symbol "v" between letters represents - in view of -.
The symbol "+" or "&" between letters represents - and -.
A slash "/" between letters represents the alternative - or -.

NOTE: Sections 100, 101, 102, 103, and 112 of the Patent Statute (Title 35 of the United States Code) are reproduced on the back of this sheet.

H. Hampton Hunter
Primary Examiner
Art Unit 353

FORM PTO-892 (REV. 3-78)

U.S. DEPARTMENT OF COMMERCE
PATENT AND TRADEMARK OFFICE

SERIAL NO. 044 836 | GROUP ART UNIT 353 | ATTACHMENT TO PAPER NUMBER 2

NOTICE OF REFERENCES CITED

APPLICANT (S)

U.S. PATENT DOCUMENTS

*		DOCUMENT NO.	DATE	NAME	CLASS	SUB-CLASS	FILING DATE IF APPROPRIATE
✓	A	3712299	1/1973	Voehl	2	24 X	
✓	B	4041940	8/1977	Frankel et al	2	24 X	
✓	C	2188718	1/1940	Jung	2	24	
✓	D	2858540	11/1958	Morrison	2	24	
✓	E	3406406	10/1968	Lutz	2	24	
✓	F	4568312	1/1978	Ledesma	2	24	
✓	G	1835295	12/1931	Glahe	2	24	
	H						
	I						
	J						
	K						

FOREIGN PATENT DOCUMENTS

*		DOCUMENT NO.	DATE	COUNTRY	NAME	CLASS	SUB-CLASS	PERTINENT SHTS. DWG	PERTINENT PP. SPEC.
	L								
	M								
	N								
	O								
	P								
	Q								

OTHER REFERENCES (Including Author, Title, Date, Pertinent Pages, Etc.)

R

EXAMINER: H Hunter | DATE: 9/7/79

* A copy of this reference is not being furnished with this office action.
(See Manual of Patent Examining Procedure, section 707.05 (a).)

35 U.S.C. 100. Definitions. When used in this title unless the context otherwise indicates —

(a) The term "invention" means invention or discovery.

(b) The term "process" means process, art or method, and includes a new use of a known process, machine, manufacture, composition of matter, or material.

(c) The terms "United States" and "this country" mean the United States of America, its territories and possessions.

(d) The word "patentee" includes not only the patentee to whom the patent was issued but also the successors in title to the patentee.

35 U.S.C. 101. Inventions patentable. Whoever invents or discovers any new and useful process, machine, manufacture, or composition of matter, or any new and useful improvement thereof, may obtain a patent therefor, subject to the conditions and requirements of this title.

35 U.S.C. 102. Conditions for patentability; novelty and loss of right to patent. A person shall be entitled to a patent unless —

(a) the invention was known or used by others in this country, or patented or described in a printed publication is this or a foreign country, before the invention thereof by the applicant for patent, or

(b) the invention was patented or described in a printed publication in this or a foreign country or in public use or on sale in this country, more than one year prior to the date of the application for patent in the United States, or

(c) he has abandoned the invention, or

(d) the invention was first patented or cause to be patented by the applicant or his legal representatives or assigns in a foreign country prior to the date of the application for patent in this country on an application filed more than twelve months before the filing of the application in the United States, or

(e) the invention was described in a patent granted on an application for patent by another filed in the United States before the invention thereof by the applicant for patent, or

(f) he did not himself invent the subject matter sought to be patented, or

(g) before the applicant's invention thereof the invention was made in this country by another who had not abandoned, suppressed, or concealed it. In determining priority of invention there shall be considered not only the respective dates of conception and reduction to practice of the invention, but also the reasonable diligence of one who was first to conceive and last to reduce to practice, from a time prior to conception by the other.

35 U.S.C. 103. Conditions for patentability; non—obvious subject matter. A patent may not be obtained though the invention is not identically disclosed or described as set forth in section 102 of this title, if the differences between the subject matter sought to be patented and the prior art are such that the subject matter as a whole would have been obvious at the time the invention was made to a person having ordinary skill in the art to which said subject matter pertains. Patentability shall not be negatived by the manner in which the invention was made.

35 U.S.C. 112. Specification. The specification shall contain a written description of the invention, and of the manner and process of making and using it, in such full, clear, concise, and exact terms as to enable any person skilled in the art to which it pertains, or with which it is most nearly connected, to make and use the same, and shall set forth the best mode contemplated by the inventor of carrying out his invention.

The specification shall conclude with one or more claims particularly pointing out and distinctly claiming the subject matter which the applicant regards as his invention. A claim may be written in independent or dependent form, and if in dependent form, it shall be construed to include all the limitations of the claim incorporated by reference into the dependent claim.

An element in a claim for a combination may be expressed as a means or step for performing a specified function without the recital of structure, material, or acts in support thereof, and such claim shall be construed to cover the corresponding structure, material, or acts described in the specification and equivalents thereof.

4

Responding to the Office Action

Think positive. Once the disappointment of the examiner's first Office action has worn off, try to pinpoint the advantages your invention has over the references he cited to reject your claims. Make a list. Check your specification and drawings to make sure these advantages really are present. There is no point in arguing about things that aren't in your application.

If the examiner objected to certain things in your specification, such as what he finds to be vague and ambiguous language, figure out how to describe your invention better. Often, examiners make these objections so a third-person reader will understand what you are saying, not because he doesn't understand it himself.

REVISING THE DRAWINGS

Examiners usually object to drawings in two ways. Often, they object on informalities, such as "lead lines are too long, shading is improper, hatching is necessary." To correct these mistakes, write a letter to the official draftsman and tell him verbatim the objections of the examiner. The drawings will not be returned to you. Instead, you will pay the Patent Office to do the work for you. Tell him not to do the work until at least one of your claims is found to be allowable and you are assured of getting your patent. It would be a waste of money to pay to have your drawings corrected if you were not granted a patent.

If the examiner has a more specific complaint, such as "Element A should be shown in section" or "lead line 22 should identify the lever, not the pivot point," you should submit a sketch, usually a photocopy of the original drawing, with the changes marked in red pen. Remember, the draftsman knows only what you tell him, so be clear in your instructions and sketches. Again, ask him not to start the work until at least one of your claims has been allowed. When he has finished the work, he'll send you a copy.

AMENDING THE CLAIMS

Now comes the crucial part, amending the claims. If you think the examiner was on solid ground and you agree with his objections and rejections, you should amend the claims by adding limitations and restricting their scope. If you feel the examiner went too far in his objections, you may decide not to change your claims. Instead, you can argue, very politely, of course, and point out his error. However, if you fail to convince him, he'll reject your application again, and this time he'll make it final.

Let's look at the Helton snow shovel from the point of view of defending the claims. Suppose the examiner applied these patents against Helton's claims: Vaslas, Catlon, and Davidson (pages 41–43).

The filing date on Vaslas (page 41) is August 1, 1978, a month and a half later than the Helton filing date. Helton should point this out to the examiner. It is not a prior invention. Also, Vaslas mounts his auxiliary handle to the backside of the blade at each top corner, while Helton uses a single swivel connection in the middle of the blade. Helton should mention this, too.

The Catlin patent (page 42) was issued in 1947, so, obviously, it can be applied against Helton's claims as a prior invention. However, as FIGS. 1 and 4 illustrate, Catlin has an adjustable handle on the main handle shank. This is interesting, but it really doesn't anticipate Helton's invention. In other words, Helton could safely tell the examiner that Catlin's invention has no bearing on his.

The Davidson patent (page 43) was issued September 27, 1977, less than a year before Helton filed his patent application. If Helton can prove that he invented his shovel before Davidson filed for his patent, the examiner cannot discredit his claims on the basis of Davidson's invention. That is, the examiner cannot use Davidson as a reference if Helton was the first inventor. This is called a "swear-back situation." (See page 47 for a more in-depth discussion of swear-back.) In addition, Davidson has a swivel-joint connection at the base of his handle, which is not the same as Helton's auxiliary-handle attachment.

When you compare the Helton shovel to the examiner's references, it becomes obvious that the difference resides in the type of joining connection and where it is mounted on the shovel. Look at Helton's claims again. This is what he says. In his response, he must convince the examiner of this.

United States Patent [19]

Vaslas

[11] **4,103,954**

[45] **Aug. 1, 1978**

[54] **SNOW SHOVEL**

[76] Inventor: **John W. Vaslas,** 282 Park St., Staten Island, N.Y. 10306

[21] Appl. No.: **787,360**

[22] Filed: **Apr. 14, 1977**

[51] **Int. Cl.**[2] **A01B 1/22;** E01H 5/02

[52] **U.S. Cl.** **294/54;** 294/58

[58] **Field of Search** .... 294/54, 57, 58, 59; 15/143 R, 144 R, 145; 16/114 R; 37/53

[56] **References Cited**

U.S. PATENT DOCUMENTS

702,097	6/1902	Haviland	294/58
911,291	2/1909	Byor	294/58
1,083,054	12/1913	Brown	294/58
1,456,879	5/1923	Newman	294/58
2,229,053	1/1941	De Vaux	37/53
2,416,414	2/1947	Spencer	294/58
3,082,554	3/1963	Steeb	294/58 X
3,751,094	8/1973	Bohler	294/58

Primary Examiner—Johnny D. Cherry
Attorney, Agent, or Firm—Norbert F. Holler

[57] **ABSTRACT**

A snow shovel having a plate-shaped scoop, a main handle and an adjustable auxiliary handle, arranged so as to enable snow to be shoveled without the user having to bend over, is disclosed. The main handle is a rod rigidly affixed to one end to the scoop and having a first hand grip at th other end. The auxiliary handle includes a pair of rods which diverge from one another in the direction from closely juxtaposed first ends to widely spaced second ends. A second hand grip is secured to the auxiliary handle rods at the first ends thereof, and respective hinges interconnect the auxiliary handle rods at their second ends to the scoop adjacent the top edge thereof. A rigid cross-brace bar, which may be medially foldable, is swivelly connected at one of its ends to the auxiliary handle rods adjacent the juncture thereof with the second hand grip and is releasably locked at its other end to the main handle rod for adjustability to different positions. The auxliary handle structure per se may be combined ith existing, conventional show shovels by providing the free ends of the auxiliary handle rods and the cross-brace bar with suitable, preferably quick-disconnect, coupling means. This abstract is not to be taken either as a complete exposition or as a limitation of the present invention, however, the full nature and extent of the invention being discernible only by reference to and for the entire disclosure.

14 Claims, 14 Drawing Figures

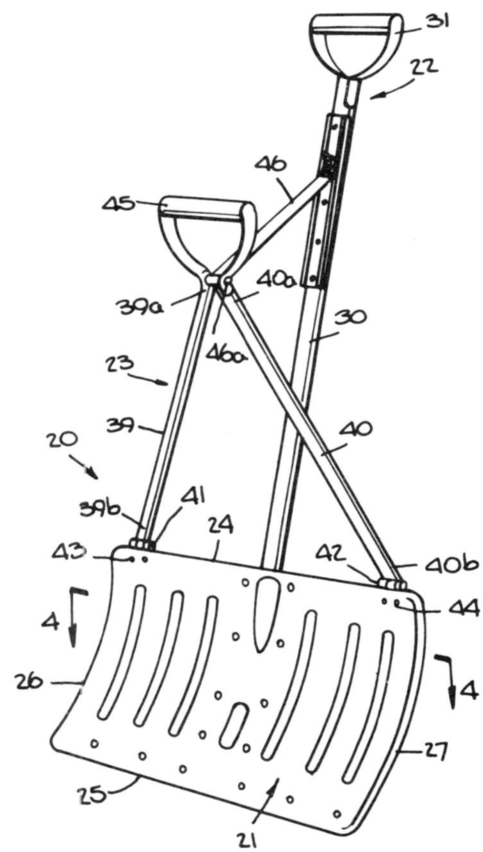

Nov. 11, 1947. J. H. CATLIN 2,430,802

AUXILIARY HAND GRIP FOR SHOVELS

Filed Aug. 6, 1945

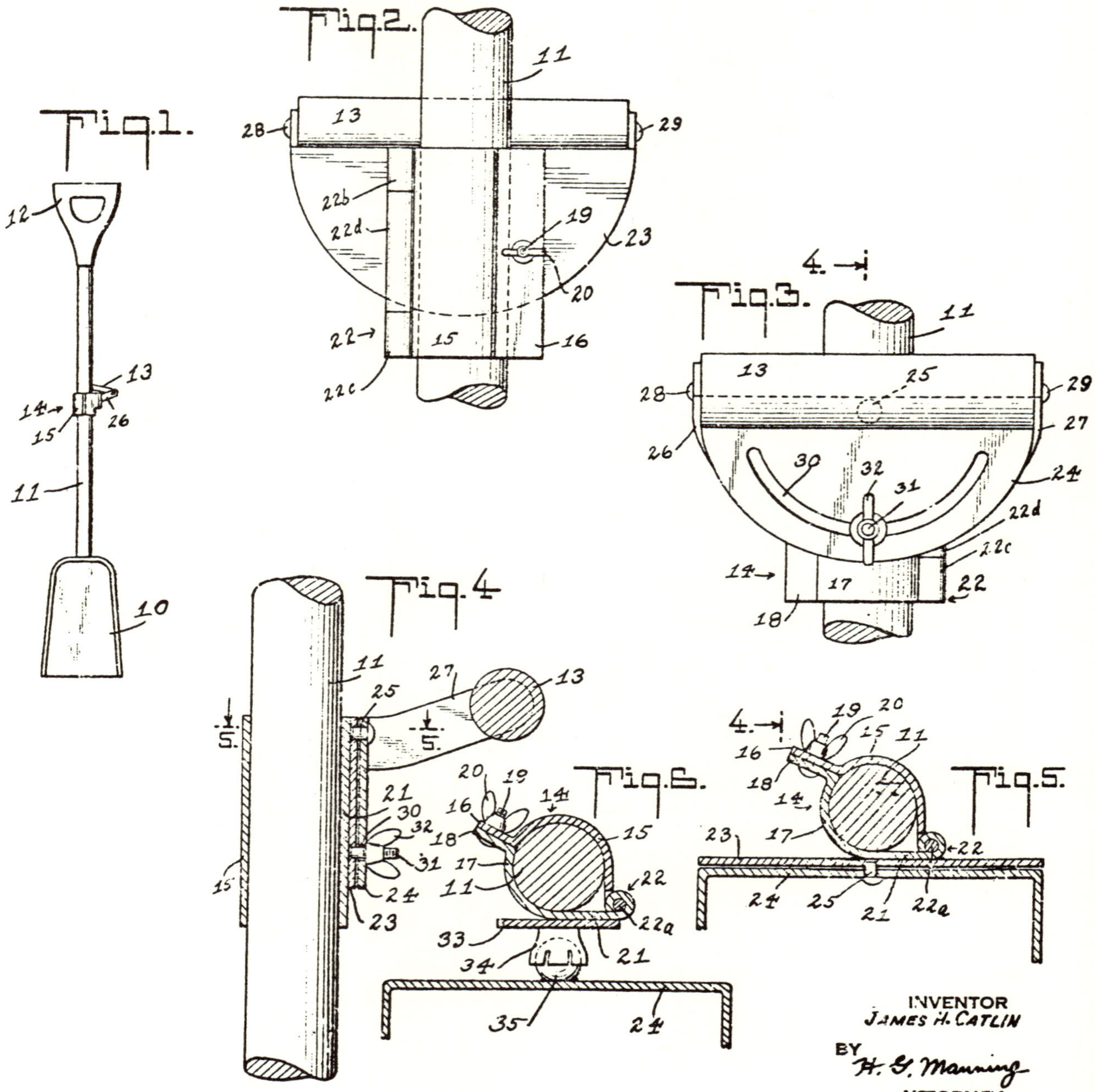

INVENTOR
JAMES H. CATLIN
BY
H. G. Manning
ATTORNEY

United States Patent [19]

Davidson

[11] **4,050,728**

[45] **Sept. 27, 1977**

[54] **SECOND HANDLE FOR ATTACHING TO A SHOVEL OR THE LIKE**

[76] Inventor: **Glenn E. Davidson,** 205 Franklin, Sublette, Kans. 67877

[21] Appl. No.: **731,465**

[22] Filed: **Oct. 12, 1976**

[51] **Int. Cl.**^{2} **B25G 3/00**

[52] **U.S. Cl.** .... **294/58;** 16/114 R; 16/115

[58] **Field of Search** .... 16/114 R, 115, 112; 294/58

[56] **References Cited**

U.S. PATENT DOCUMENTS

911,291	2/1909	Byor	294/58
1,374,061	4/1921	Coleman	294/58
1,586,056	5/1926	Walsh	294/58
2,047,485	7/1936	McBrady	16/115 UX

FOREIGN PATENT DOCUMENTS

410,274	3/1925	Germany	294/58
915,288	1/1963	United Kingdom	294/58

Primary Examiner—Andrew V. Kundrat
Attorney, Agent, or Firm—Edwin H. Crabtree; John H. Widdowson

[57] **ABSTRACT**

A second handle for attaching to a shovel, or various types of garden tools having a handle attached thereto. The second handle having a universal joint at one end for attaching to the handle of the shovel. The universal joint allowing the user to pivot the second handle in various directions on the shovel for ease in lifting, pushing or pulling the material being handled.

4 Claims, 4 Drawing Figures

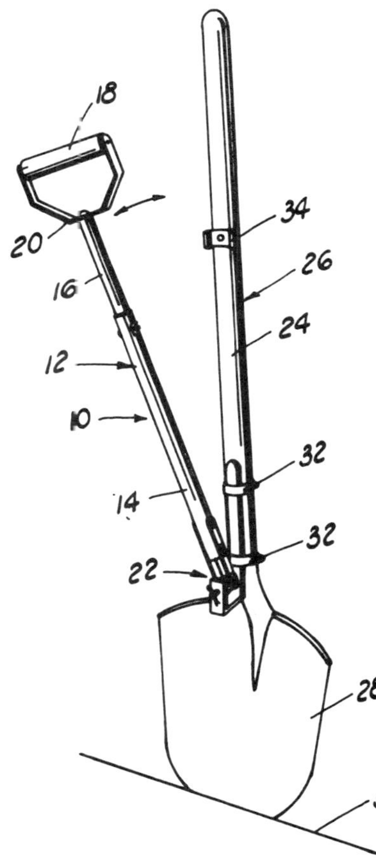

FORMALIZING YOUR RESPONSE

Now, tell the examiner exactly what you want to change. To amend the specification, tell him what words must be inserted and what words must be stricken out. Here's an example:

```
In the Specification

Page 4, line 6 after "snow"
insert–shovel–. Cancel "event."
```

You can see why it is so important to keep an exact copy of your application.

Rewrite your claims by underlining the words to be added and bracketing the words to be deleted. If you want to cancel an entire claim, just say so. Tell the examiner, "Cancel claim 6." If your typewriter doesn't have brackets, put them in by hand. Whenever you rewrite a claim, you must put the word "amended" after the original claim number. If you rewrite the claim yet another time, put "twice amended" in parentheses after the original claim number. Here's an example:

```
In the Claims

Rewrite claim 1 as follows:

1. (Amended) In combination:

  A shovel having a blade portion
and a handle secured to [each] said
blade portion. . . .
```

There is another way to amend your claims. You can make minor corrections, such as spelling and punctuation changes, and add up to five additional words, in the same way you revise the specification—that is, by telling the examiner what words are to be added and what words are to be deleted. If you don't follow these instructions when you amend your claims, your changes will not be made.

If you add an entirely new claim, give it the next higher number. For instance, if your last claim is number 8 and you want to add a new claim, label it number 9. Remember, for your initial $65 filing fee, you are entitled to one independent claim and nine dependent claims. So, unless you cancel other claims, additional claims may cost you extra money if you exceed your limit.

REMARKS

Here is where you tell the examiner what you've done. Tell him you are asking the official draftsman to make certain changes in drawings, subject to his approval and upon the allowance of one of your claims. Tell him that you have corrected the informalities in the specification. Tell him what claims you have added, what claims you have cancelled, what claims you want him to reconsider, and what claims you have amended. This lets the examiner know at a glance that you have made a serious, bona fide attempt to advance the application to a successful conclusion.

Next, tell the examiner how the references he cited differ from your claims. Explain exactly how your invention is different from these prior inventions. Explain what elements in your claims are not present in the prior patents. Remember, it is in the claims that your patent must be different from previous inventions. You must make this clear.

After you point out how your invention differs from the examiner's references, you must convince him that these changes are important, would not readily occur to one skilled in the art, and therefore amount to invention. Hence, the claims should be allowed. Tell him so.

Lastly, ask the examiner politely to reconsider your claims in view of your remarks and the amendments you have made. Sign your name and put the title "Applicant" or "Inventor" below it.

Type your response, double-spaced. If you can't type, have a professional do it for you. Make it as easy as possible for the examiner to read it (and to agree with your arguments). Set up the first sheet of your response like this:

In the U.S. Patent Office

Inventor: Wayland Helton Examiner: John D. Cherry

Title: Snow shovel Art Group: 290

Serial No.: 916,140 Amendment

Filing Date: June 16, 1978

Commissioner of Patents

Washington, DC 20231

Sir:

In response to the Office Action dated 10 June 1979, please amend this Application as follows:

CERTIFICATE OF MAILING

Below your name make a new heading, "Certificate of Mailing," and type this line beneath it: "This is to certify that on this date I deposited this correspondence with the U.S. Postal Service as first class mail in an envelope addressed to the Commissioner of Patents, Washington, D.C. 20231." Then sign your name again and write the date.

Check to see if you have enclosed a letter to the draftsman with instructions on correcting your drawing (if necessary) and payment for any extra claims you might be adding. Don't forget the self-addressed, stamped postcard that the Patent Office will return to you upon receipt of your response and will be your proof that you did indeed respond in time.

Revival of Abandonment

If you fail to respond to the Office action within the time the examiner sets, your application will be abandoned. Remember, the maximum time for response is six months, although the Patent Office may set a shorter time limit. You usually have three months to respond to an Office action. If your application is abandoned, you may be able to revive it by submitting a Petition to Revive, in which you state the reasons for the delay. Here is a sample revival petition:

Inventor: Wayland Helton

Filing Date: June 16, 1978

Title: Snow shovel

Date: September 30, 1979

Serial No.: 916,140

Commissioner of Patents

Washington, DC 20231

Sir:

In response to the Patent Office letter dated 18 September 1979, in which the examiner says the applicant's patent application has been abandoned because the applicant failed to respond within the time limit established for response, the applicant claims the delay was unavoidable for these reasons:

[State the reasons for your delay.]

Name

Date

Usually, acceptable reasons for a delay are hospitalization, mail delays, extended absences from home, etc. There is a $15 petition fee, which you must enclose with your letter. If you haven't already filed the delinquent response, enclose that, too.

Swear-Back

Swear-back is officially known as a Rule 131 Declaration of Prior Invention to overcome a cited patent or publication that was filed or published less than a year before you filed your application. This is how it works: If the examiner applies a prior patent against your claims, and you can prove that you invented before the date the other patent was issued, the examiner will have to remove the other invention as a reference. Swear-back only works if the other inventor did not claim the same things you did. If two inventors have the same claims, they are in an interference situation (see page 48).

Your swear-back is a separate paper that you include with your response. Use the same heading you use for your response (see page 45), except instead of heading it "Amendment" head it "Rule 131 Declaration." Supply the examiner with the facts that establish you as the first inventor, and include any drawings or records that will verify your arguments.

Final Rejection

When the examiner receives your response, he will reexamine your application, then notify you if he still rejects your claims or makes other objections or requirements.

Upon the second and subsequent examinations of your application, the examiner may make his rejection final. When he does this, he will again state his reasons. What can you do? If he rejects your claims again, you can appeal (see pages 49–52). Or, you can respond with another argument and amendments within the time limit he sets—usually three months. If you don't respond and your changes aren't accepted within this time limit, your application will be abandoned. If the examiner fails to answer within the time limit, don't risk abandonment. File a Notice of Appeal to keep your application alive. If the examiner makes objections that do not involve your claims, you can petition the Commissioner of Patents or comply with the necessary changes. Again, you must respond within the time limit. You can also set up an interview to plead your case in person, but this does not remove the necessity of a written response. However, interviews are very helpful as the examiner will make sure you understand your problem and often he will help you solve it.

Interferences

An interference is a proceeding in which the Patent Office determines which of two or more inventors is entitled to a patent. First of all, there is only a 1 percent chance that you will find yourself in an interference situation. Secondly, this is a very complex process, so you are well advised to find an attorney to help you with it.

Only one patent will be granted on an invention. It will go to the person who first reduced the invention to practice unless: another party conceived the invention first and was continuously diligent in working toward its reduction to practice from a time before the first party's conception of the invention until the first party reduced the invention to practice *or* unless the first party to reduce the invention to practice thereafter abandoned, suppressed, or concealed the invention.

Several definitions are in order.

Conception of an invention is the formation of a definite and permanent idea of the complete and operative invention as it is to be applied in practice. Sketches and a written description are evidence of conception.

Reduction to practice occurs when the invention is in practical form, such as a working model. The filing of an application is a *constructive* reduction; if you file your application before you build a working model or put your invention into practical form in another way, you can use the filing date as the date you reduced your invention to practice.

Diligence is a reasonable effort directed at embodying the invention in physical form or in filing a patent application.

Abandonment is the intentional or unintentional surrender of the right to patent protection.

Suppression or *concealment* is the withholding of the invention from the public until another party discloses the invention to the public.

The *senior party* is the applicant with the earliest filing date. The *junior party* is the applicant with the more recent filing date.

The junior party has the burden of proving that he, not the senior party, should be awarded the patent. Both parties must supply proof of when they made their inventions. If a party does not supply evidence suggesting otherwise, his filing date stands as the date he made his invention. Interference cases are decided upon by a three-member Board of Patent Interferences, which bases its decision on written briefs and a hearing.

Since interference proceedings are very complicated, time-consuming, and costly, the parties involved are often willing to settle their differences on their own. An agreement like this usually occurs after each party has filed his preliminary statement, in which he states, under oath, that he indeed made the invention, whether or not he made it in the United States, and other facts that will establish him as the first inventor. At that point, it is usually clear who the prevailing party is, providing the allegations can be proven.

Don't panic if you get caught up in an interference situation; you may find that the other party is willing to license your invention or buy it from you. All things considered, this may be preferable to marketing your invention yourself.

5

Appeals

If the examiner rejects your claims in his Final Action, you can appeal. The first step is to submit a Notice of Appeal within the time limit the examiner specifies in the Final Rejection. In a letter headed like the one on page 45, state that you are appealing the adverse decision of the examiner in his Final Rejection (give the date of the Rejection) in rejecting your claims (give the claim numbers). That's all you have to say. Enclose the required $50 Notice of Appeal fee, along with a self-addressed postcard so you can prove the date you filed your notice. You then have two months to file the Appeal Briefs. If you don't file the briefs and an additional $50 within the two months, your appeal will be dismissed.

APPEAL BRIEFS

About 60 percent of patent applications mature into patents. The rest fail for lack of patentability, abandonment, or because the applicant drops his prosecution when he discovers his invention is not marketable or profitable. If your application has been rejected, but if you think your invention really does have patentable merit and commercial potential, continue with your appeal. Statistics show that you have a 24 percent chance of winning. To win, you must have a positive attitude, the determination to beat the examiner who "just won't be reasonable," and the ability to convince the three members of the Board of Appeals that you are right and the examiner is wrong.

Formalizing the Appeal Brief

Members of the Board of Appeals are exceptionally talented people who were formerly senior examiners. They are very busy and don't have time to wade through the files on your patent application. Instead, they rely on your brief, the examiner's answer to your brief, and your reply to that. So, it is essential that your brief is logical and easy to follow.

First, your brief should have a table of contents. Here's an example:

Table of Contents

Introduction

This is what the Board members read first. In precise terms, let them know what's going on. Write something like this: "This is an appeal from the decision dated 22 October 1980 of the primary examiner FINALLY rejecting claims 1, 3, 8, 10, and 11. A response to this rejection was received by the Patent Office 15 December 1980. The examiner indicates that this response overcame his rejection that the claims were indefinite under 35 U.S.C. 112. However, the examiner persists in his FINAL rejection of the claims as being unpatentable over the references cited under 35 U.S.C. 103. Hence, Notice of Appeal (and $50 fee) was mailed 19 January 1981. An oral hearing is/*is not* desired."

The Problem

Here you discuss the problem that gave rise to the invention. Take this section right from the background section in your application.

Applicant's Solution

Use the summary of the invention from your application. If you have made your invention, include photographs, labelling the different parts with the same numbers you used in your drawings. Photographs are an attraction because they prove the device was actually built. Besides, examiners and Board members are used to seeing drawings, so photographs are a pleasant change. Include the drawings also, though; they're useful.

The Claims on Appeal

Copy the claims verbatim, just as they stood when the examiner rejected them.

The Examiner's Final Rejection

Copy it verbatim.

Examiner's Rebuttal of Applicant's Remarks

If you responded to the Final Rejection (and you should have), and if the examiner responded to your arguments, tell the Board members about his rebuttal.

The References

Mention the prior patents and explain how they operate. Subtly imply how they differ from your invention, but don't overdo it. This is supposed to be a factual description, not a defensive argument.

The Issue

Now you must convince the Board members that your invention really is different from the references the examiner has cited. Tell them how your invention differs from these prior patents and the advantages it has over them. Explain that even if all of these references were combined, they still would not do what your invention does. Convince them that you have indeed invented a new and useful device.

Conclusion

This is the windup. Simply ask the Board to agree with you that your claims should be allowed and that your appeal should be granted.

Sign your appeal brief, make three copies, and mail it. Don't forget the $50 briefs fee and a self-addressed, stamped postcard to verify receipt.

Response and Reply

About six weeks after you file your brief, call the examiner and ask him if he has had a chance to read it. If he has, offer to cancel certain claims if he will allow others. If he hasn't received your brief yet, give him the mailing date and ask when he would expect to receive it. Call him back then.

The examiner must write an extensive answer to your briefs. Then he has to present your case before an unofficial board of three examiners. If he thinks a Board of Appeals would agree with you and he would lose, he'll allow your claims. He doesn't want a loss on his record. If he still thinks your application should be rejected and that he can defend his decision before the Board of Appeals, he will write an Examiner's Answer in response to your briefs. He will explain his interpretation of your claims, the references as he is applying them against your invention, and the grounds for his rejection.

You have 20 days to file a reply. It must be confined to new points the examiner raised in his answer. The board members will read it for your rebuttal of his new points. However, the examiner usually does not raise new points, so you won't need to reply.

Now, wait to hear. Should you receive a negative response, you do have recourse in the U.S. District Court for the District of Columbia or in the U.S. Court of Customs and Patent Appeals. However, don't try to tackle these courts by yourself. Get a lawyer.

6

Patent Granted

When your patent is found to be allowable, the Patent Office will send you a Notice of Allowance, which informs you that upon payment of the issue fee of $100 plus $2 per sheet of drawings and $10 per printed page of specification, you will be granted a patent. A few weeks later, the Patent Office will send you an issue slip, which gives the date of issuance and your patent number. Barring delays, the Office should mail your patent on the date of issuance. If you've sold your patent, and the new owner has recorded the assignment with the Patent Office, you can ask that the patent be mailed to him. You can order "soft" copies, photocopies of the entire patent except the front cover, for 50 cents each. Be sure to give the patent number when ordering. Address correspondence to the Commissioner of Patents, Washington, D.C. 20231.

FILING ADDITIONAL APPLICATIONS

During the prosecution of your patent application the examiner might reject your claims by stating, "Claims 1–4 are drawn to handle structure and claims 5–8 are drawn to a process or method. Since only one invention is allowed in each application, restriction is required." If you elected claims 1–4 in your original application, you may file a duplicate application with claims 5–8 for a second patent. This application is called a divisional application and if filed while the original is still pending, will bear the original filing date in overcoming references the examiner may apply against the second application.

If the examiner in the original application rejects claims 5–8 as relating to subject matter not properly or adequately disclosed or described in the application, you may continue prosecuting your original or parent application with claims 1–4. You cannot add new subject matter to the already filed application, but you can file a continuation-in-part (CIP) application. This means that if you wish to pursue the subject matter of claims 5–8 in a second application, you may, but you must overcome the examiner's objection with a revised application in which you describe in more detail the subject matter of claims 5–8 which the examiner objected to in the original application. You may also include improvements or changes from your original embodiments that you developed since the first application was filed. You should file a CIP application before the first application becomes a patent, to get the benefit of its filing date, although the new subject matter gets the date of the second filing.

There is a third type of additional application you may wish to file. Suppose things are going badly in the prosecution of the original application and you received a FINAL office action with no claims allowed. You finally figure out an argument and change in claim language that seems to convince the examiner, except for one thing: You have no explanation or excuse why it was not earlier presented. A refiled or continuation application is in order. This gives you a fresh start, and your new arguments and changes will be considered by the examiner. In all instances where you file later applications co-pending with the original application, this fact should be stated in the later application so the examiner can relate and compare the two applications.

Declarations for additional co-pending applications are different from that for the parent application. A sample declaration follows:

Declaration in division or continuation application.

As a below named inventor, I hereby declare that:

My residence, post office address and citizenship are as stated below next to my name; that

I verily believe I am the original, first and sole inventor (if only one name is listed below) or a joint inventor (if plural inventors are named below) of the invention entitled: ——————— described and claimed in the attached specification; that this application discloses and claims only subject matter disclosed in my or our pending applicaton Serial No. ———————, filed ———————; that

I do not know and do not believe the same was ever known or used in the United States of America before my or our invention thereof, or patented or described in any printed publication in any country before my or our invention thereof or more than one year prior to said prior application, that the same was not in public use or on sale in the United States of America more than one year prior to said prior application, that said invention has not been patented or made the subject of an inventor's certificate issued before the date of said prior application in any country foreign to the United States of America on an application filed by me or my legal representatives or assigns more than twelve months prior to said application, that I acknowledge my duty to disclose information of which I am aware which is material to the examination of this application, and that no application for patent or inventor's certificate on said invention has been filed in any country foreign to the United States of America by me or my legal representatives or assigns, except as follows: ———————.

I hereby declare that all statements made herein of my own knowledge are true and that all statements made on information and belief are believed to be true; and further that these statements were made with the knowledge that willful false statements and the like so made are punishable by fine or imprisonment, or both, under Section 1001 of Title 18 of the United States Code and that such willful false statements may jeopardize the validity of the application or any patent issued thereon.

Full name of sole or first Inventor ———————

———————————————

Inventor's signature ———————————

Date: ———————.

7

Design Patents

Design patents apply to new, original, and ornamental designs for articles of manufacture. They protect the appearance of an article, not its function. Lamps, containers, tires, automobile accessories, furniture, household items, games, toys, and jewelry are commonly the subjects of design patent applications.

There are samples of design patents on pages 56–58. As you look at them, keep in mind that a design is not ornamental if it conforms to functional considerations. If your design is based on the shape of an article, you must stress its decorative, not its functional, features. Surface engravings are not considered to be designs.

THE APPLICATION

The arrangement of documents for a design application is as follows:

(a) Preamble, stating name of the applicant and title of the design.
(b) Description of the figure or figures of the drawing.
(c) Description, if any.
(d) One claim only, followed by applicant's signature.
(e) Signed declaration of applicant.

The filing fee for a design application is $20. When the application is allowed, you will be given the option of 3½, 7, or 14 years for the life of the patent. The issue fee for 3½ years is $10, for 7 years $20, and for 14 years $30.

256,955
DENTAL FLOSS HOLDER
Elmer T. Rogers, 1195 Lindberg Dr., Deptford, N.J. 08096
Filed Feb. 16, 1978, Ser. No. 878,242
Term of patent 14 years
Int. Cl. D28—*03*
U.S. Cl. D28—64

256,857
FOLDABLE CHAIR
Roger Tallon, Paris, France, assignor to Design Programmes S.A., Paris, France
Filed Jul. 27, 1978, Ser. No. 928,406
Claims priority, application France, Feb. 3, 1978, 78 76321
Term of patent 14 years
Int. Cl. D6—*01*
U.S. Cl. D6—56

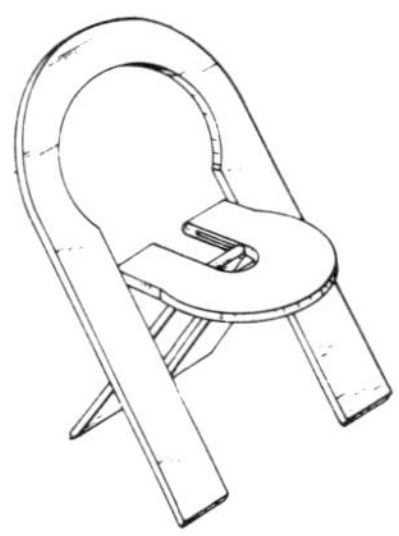

255,912
DOLLHOUSE
Milo G. Chapman, Newberg, and David E. Christie, Aurora, both of Oreg., assignors to Dura-Craft, Inc., Aurora, Oreg.
Filed Jun. 30, 1978, Ser. No. 921,362
Term of patent 14 years
Int. Cl. D21—*01*
U.S. Cl. D21—114

256,933
TOY FIGURE
Lawrence T. Jones, Playa Del Rey, and Robert S. Lee, Westlake, both of Calif., assignors to California R & D Center
Filed Feb. 1, 1979, Ser. No. 8,741
Term of patent 14 years
Int. Cl. D21—*01*
U.S. Cl. D21—166

256,892
FLOOR CLOCK
John Boukma, Grandville, Mich., assignor to Howard Miller Clock Company, Zeeland, Mich.
Filed Jun. 6, 1978, Ser. No. 913,124
Term of patent 14 years
Int. Cl. D10—*01*
U.S. Cl. D10—16

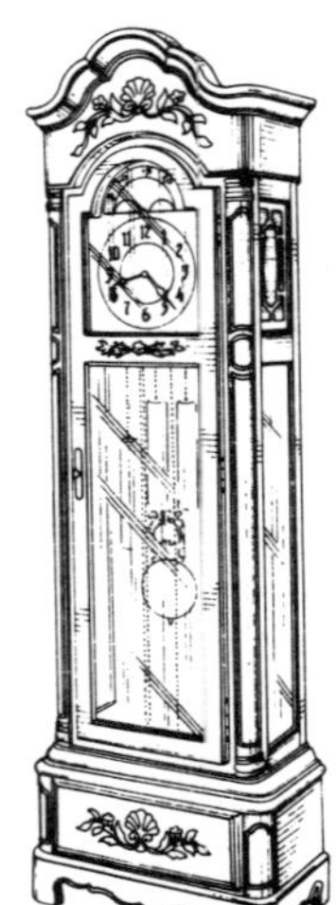

255,855
PICTURE FRAME
Rudolf A. Glogovcsan, 17701 Miranda St., Encino, Calif. 91316
Filed Nov. 6, 1978, Ser. No. 957,879
Term of patent 14 years
Int. Cl. D6—*07*
U.S. Cl. D6—235

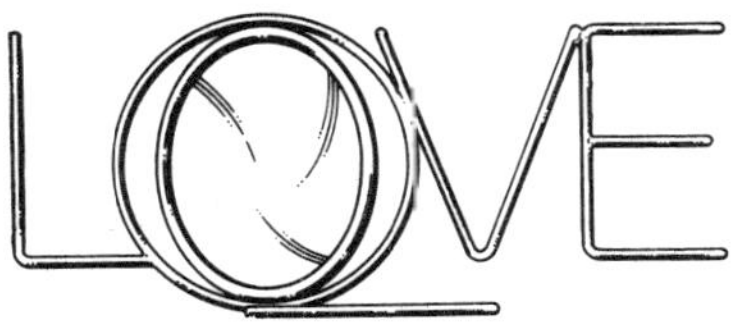

256,854
ELEPHANT BUNK BED
Angus J. Bruce, 398 W. Broadway, New York, N.Y. 10012
Filed Jun. 12, 1978, Ser. No. 914,914
Term of patent 14 years
Int. Cl. D6—*01*
U.S. Cl. D6—5

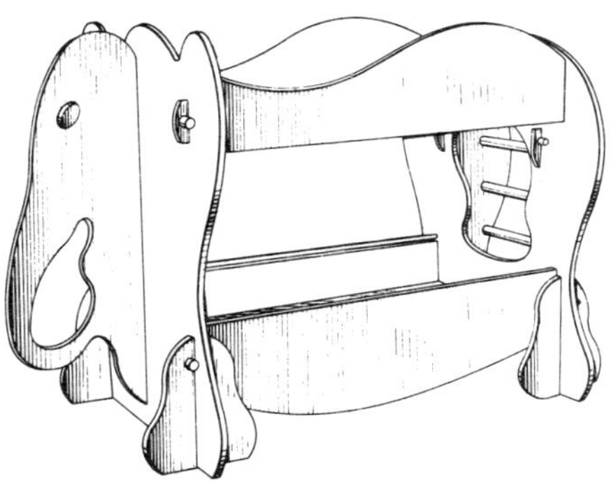

255,865
TRASH CAN COVER
Robert G. Hartman, and Clayton J. Ammondson, both of Reidsville, N.C., assignors to Zarn, Inc., Reidsville, N.C.
Filed Feb. 13, 1978, Ser. No. 877,424
Term of patent 14 years
Int. Cl. D7—*07*
U.S. Cl. D7—194

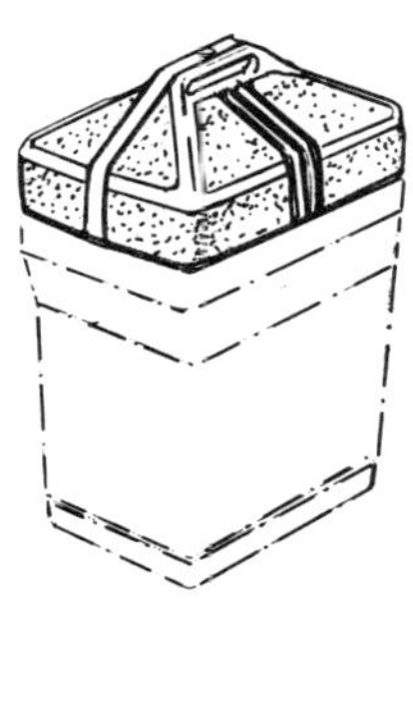

256,900
STATUETTE
Wayne Walter, R.D. 2, Box 180, Endicott, N.Y. 13760
Filed Apr. 2, 1976, Ser. No. 673,121
Term of patent 14 years
Int. Cl. D11—*02*
U.S. Cl. D11—157

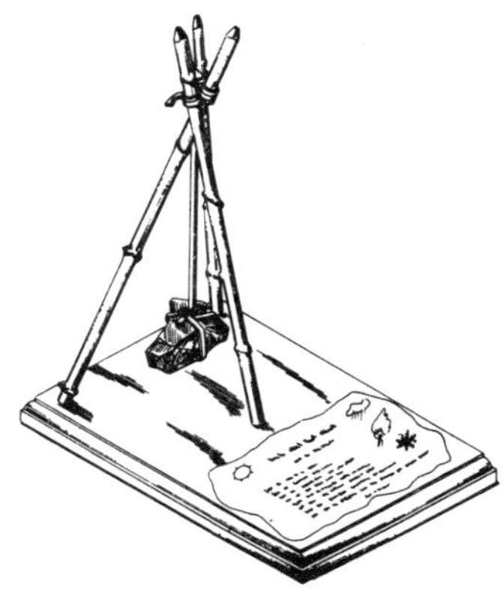

255,918
FISH LURE
William E. Hogreff, 295 D St., Apt. B, Chula Vista, Calif. 92010
Filed May 4, 1978, Ser. No. 902,998
Term of patent 14 years
Int. Cl. D22—*05*
U.S. Cl. D22—27

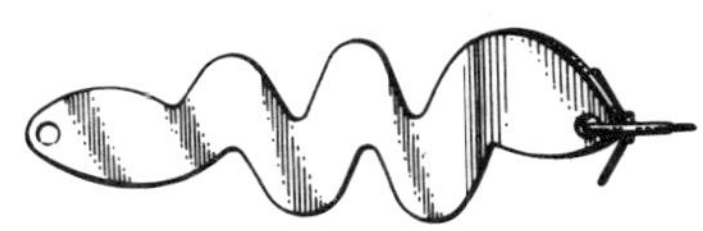

256,938
BALL PADDLE FOR TABLE GAME
Bertrand Castelli, c/o Myron Salisian, 251 S. Lake Ave., Suite 701, Pasadena, Calif. 91101
Filed Sep. 25, 1978, Ser. No. 945,183
Term of patent 14 years
Int. Cl. D21—*01*
U.S. Cl. D21—213

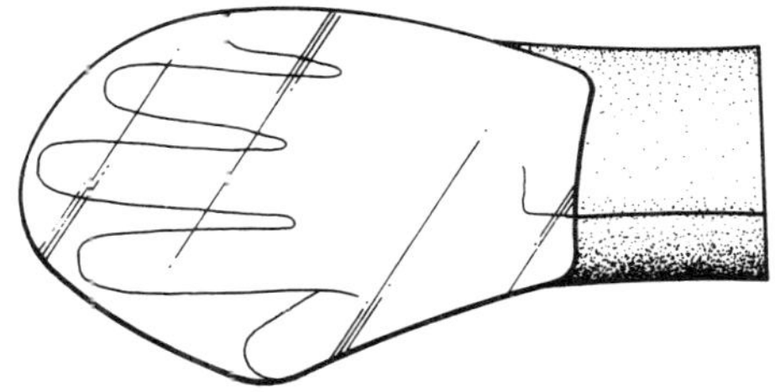

256,936
SHUTTLECOCK
Frank W. Popplewell, Saffron Walden, England, assignor to Dunlop Limited, London, England
Filed Oct. 27, 1978, Ser. No. 955,363
Claims priority, application United Kingdom, May 20, 1978, 984687/78
Term of patent 14 years
Int. Cl. D21—*02*
U.S. Cl. D21—207

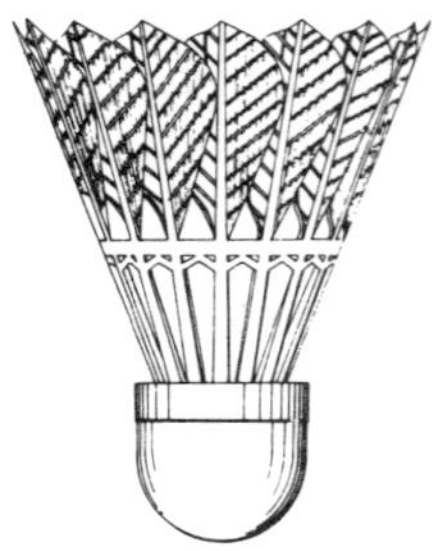

255,863
TRANSPORTABLE OUTDOOR BARBECUE GRILL
Ben F. Futch, P.O. Box 129, Valdosta, Ga. 31601
Filed Jun. 21, 1978, Ser. No. 917,680
Term of patent 14 years
Int. Cl. D7—*02*
U.S. Cl. D7—108

256,957
ANIMAL HABITAT
Fritz Jüstl, Starkenburgring 5, D-6057 Dietzenbach, Fed. Rep. of Germany
Filed Mar. 29, 1978, Ser. No. 891,354
Claims priority, application Fed. Rep. of Germany, Sep. 29, 1977, 510057
Term of patent 14 years
Int. Cl. D30—*02*
U.S. Cl. D30—1

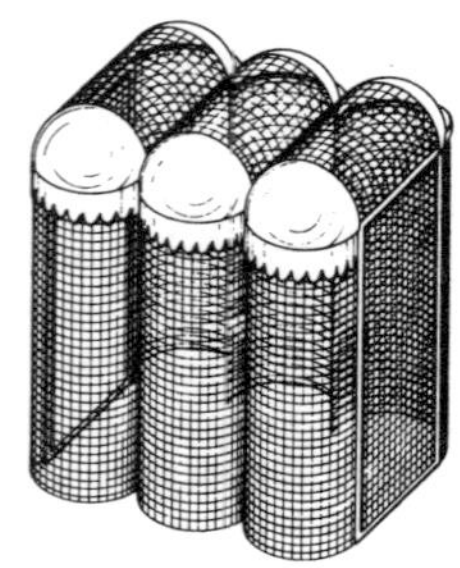

255,866
BOTTLE OPENER
Mihail Panos, 600 N. Harbor Blvd., La Habra, Calif. 90631
Filed Oct. 10, 1978, Ser. No. 949,775
Term of patent 14 years
Int. Cl. D08—*99*
U.S. Cl. D8—38

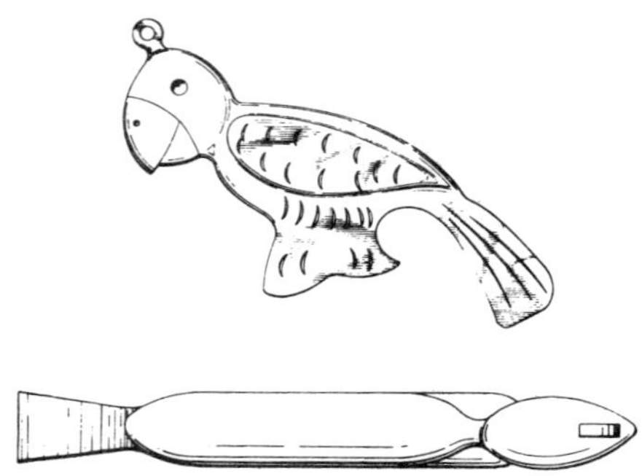

255,848
BED HEADBOARD
New Melbourne F. Smith, Jr., Rte. 10, Box 879, Hickory, N.C. 28601
Filed Oct. 30, 1978, Ser. No. 956,210
Term of patent 14 years
Int. Cl. D6—*01*
U.S. Cl. D6—79

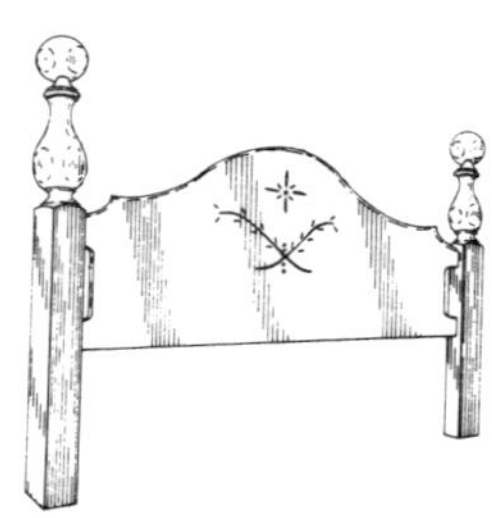

A SAMPLE DESIGN PATENT

Let's look at design patent number Des. 184,640, granted to George Roethel, Jr., March 17, 1959, shown on page 60. It is for a device that unwinds the tear strip from a coffee can. Usually, coffee cans have keys that can be pulled off, inserted over the end of the tear strip, and rotated to peel the strip off to remove the lid. On large cans, this is very time-consuming work, and the roll often slips sideways and the leverage against the can is destroyed.

On the Roethel can opener, a snap-on on the top brackets keeps the crank in alignment at all times, and the tear strip, as it is removed, stays in a compact roll. A slot in the arm permits the crank to move away from the can as it rolls up the strip. The crank peels off the tear strip from the can easily and quickly.

As you can see, the can opener has functional advantages, and Roethel probably could have obtained a utility patent. (Most patents, such as the ones we discussed in the main part of this book, are utility patents and stress function.) However, since design patents are easier, faster to obtain, and cheaper, Roethel chose to go that route.

In setting forth your arguments for a design patent, you do not mention function at all. In the case of the Roethel can opener, the arguments would center on the overall appearance, as being pleasing to the eye. The simplicity of the lines would also be mentioned.

Notice how short the specification in a design patent application is. Also, you can only have one claim for a design patent, and in it you always refer to the invention "as shown." Sometimes, the examiner will suggest that you use more descriptive language in the specification and that you add the words "and described" in the claim. This means the design patent is granted on the pleasing and decorative appearance of the item in the drawing, together with any limitation in the specification.

The appearance of the drawing is all-important. Notice the phantom lines of the coffee can. These show that it is not part of the invention. Its presence shows the relationship of the can opener to the can. The shading on the can opener gives it life. You can almost see it in three dimensions, not as a flat object on a piece of paper. In the Roethel patent, only a perspective view is shown. However, this is not typical. The design patent rules require a sufficient number of views to constitute a complete disclosure of the appearance of the article, with appropriate shading to show the character or contour of the surfaces represented. Otherwise, the mechanics of design patent drawings are the same as those for utility patents.

United States Patent Office

Des. 184,640
Patented Mar. 17, 1959

184,640

TEAR STRIP CAN OPENER

George Roethel, Jr., San Diego, Calif.

Application July 22, 1957, Serial No. 47,032

Term of patent 7 years

(Cl. D44—29)

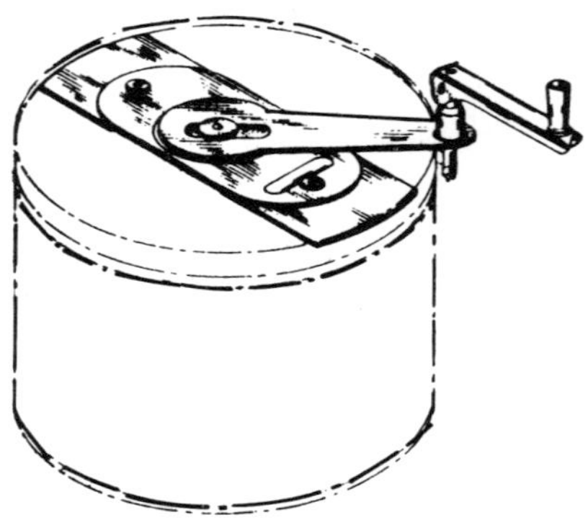

The figure is a perspective view of a tear strip can opener showing my new design, with a can shown in broken lines for purposes of illustration.

I claim:

The ornamental design for a tear strip can opener, as shown and described.

References Cited in the file of this patent

UNITED STATES PATENTS

921,250	Hough	May 11, 1909
1,759,364	Quigg	May 20, 1930
2,625,294	Bodin et al.	Jan. 13, 1953
2,734,896	Pollard	Mar. 20, 1956

8

Plant Patents

The Patent Office began issuing plant patents in 1930, in order to give agriculture the same protection it gives to industry with utility and design patents. Let's look at the portion of the patent law that applies to plants:

> Whoever invents or discovers and asexually reproduces any distinct and new variety of plant, including cultivated sports, mutants, hybrids, and newly found seedlings, other than a tuber propagated plant or a plant found in an uncultivated state, may obtain a patent therefor, subject to the conditions and requirements set forth.
>
> The provisions relating to patents for inventions shall apply to patents for plants, except as otherwise provided.
>
> In the case of a plant patent the grant shall be of the right to exclude others from asexually reproducing the plant or selling or using the plant so reproduced.

Notice that the plant must be cultivated in order to be patentable. Plants growing freely in the wild cannot be patented.

THE APPLICATION

Here are the Patent Office guidelines for filing an application for a plant patent.

Specification

The specification must contain as full and complete a disclosure as possible of the plant and the characteristics thereof that distinguish the same over related known varieties, and its antecedents, and must particularly point out where and in what manner the variety of plant has been asexually reproduced. In the case of a newly found plant, the specification must particularly point out the location and character of the area where the plant was discovered.

Two copies of the specification (including the claim) must be submitted, but only one need be signed and executed; the second copy may be a legible carbon copy of the original.

Claim

The claim shall be in formal terms to the new and distinct variety of the specified plant as described and illustrated, and may also recite the principal distinguishing characteristics. More than one claim is not permitted.

Drawings

Plant patent drawings are not mechanical drawings and should be artistically and competently executed. Figure numbers and reference characters need not be employed unless required by the examiner. The drawing must disclose all the distinctive characteristics of the plant capable of visual representation.

The drawing *may* be in color and when color is a distinguishing characteristic of the new variety, the drawing *must* be in color. Two copies of color drawings must be submitted. Color drawings may be made either in permanent water color or oil, or in lieu thereof may be photographs made by color photography or properly colored on sensitized paper. Permanently mounted color photographs are acceptable. The paper in any case must correspond in size, weight and quality to the paper required for other drawings. Nonpermanently mounted copies will be correctly mounted at applicant's expense.

Specimens

The applicant may be required to furnish specimens of the plant, or its flower or fruit, in a quantity and at a time in its stage of growth as may be designated, for study and inspection. Such specimens, properly packed, must be forwarded in conformity with instructions furnished to the applicant. When it is not possible to forward such specimens, plants must be made available for official inspection where grown.

Examination

Applications may be submitted by the Patent and Trademark Office to the Department of Agriculture for study and report.

Affidavits or declarations from qualified agricultural or horticultural experts regarding the novelty and distinctiveness of the variety of plant may be received when the need of such affidavits or declarations is indicated.

Patented June 15, 1943 **Plant Pat. 591**

UNITED STATES PATENT OFFICE

591

ROSE PLANT

Francis Meilland, Tassin-les-Lyon, France, assignor to The Conrad-Pyle Company, West Grove, Pa.

Application July 15, 1942, Serial No. 451,039

1 Claim. (Cl. 47—61)

The present invention relates to a new and distinct variety of hybrid tea rose plant, a seedling resulting from a definite effort to produce an improvement in this class of roses.

The primary features of this new variety which connote its distinctive advance over existing types are the exceptional vigor and enduring quality of its foliage and the character of its bloom, first in respect to its size; second, its perfection of form; and third, with respect to its exquisite blend of coloring, more particularly apparent in the accompanying illustration of a specimen thereof.

The following is a detail description of the new variety, color terminology being in accord with Ridgway's Color Standard:

Type: Hardy; bush; outdoor; seedling; for cut flowers and garden decoration.

Class: Hybrid tea.

Propagation: Holds its distinguishing characteristics through succeeding propagations by budding.

Flower

Locality where grown: West Grove, Pennsylvania.

Flowers borne: Singly to stem on strong, medium long stems.

Quantity of bloom: Abundant outdoors.

Continuity: Intermittent, almost continuous.

Fragrance: Moderate; tea.

Bud:

Peduncle.—Medium long; heavy; erect; stiff; Dark Citrine, Plate IV; rough. Prickles—moderately few, Garnet-Brown, Plate I.

Before calyx breaks.—*Size*—large. *Form*—globular with an inconspicuous neck; with foliaceous appendages on the surface of the bud; with bristle-like foliaceous parts extending beyond the tip of the bud equal to about one-fourth of its length.

As calyx breaks.—Pale Lemon Yellow, Plate IV, flushed with Nopal Red, Plate I.

As first petal opens.—*Size*—large. *Form*—ovoid. *Color*—Outside—Lemon Yellow base to Martius Yellow edge, Plate IV. Inside—Lemon Yellow base to Martius Yellow edge, Plate IV, and tipped Shrimp Pink, Plate I. *Opening*—opens up well.

Bloom:

Size when fully open.—Large; five to five and one-half inches.

Petalage.—Very double; from fifty to fifty-five petals arranged regularly.

Form.—*Cupped*; high centers; globular at first; becoming cupped and high centered; petals remaining at first tightly rolled inward; becoming later, at maturity, loosely rolled outward.

Petals: Leathery; inside and outside satiny.

Shape.—Outside—oval; scalloped with apex flat with one notch. Intermediate—ovate; scalloped with one notch. Inside—ovate; scalloped with one notch.

This description of a newly opened flower was made from a rose grown outdoors during the month of November, 1941, at West Grove, Pennsylvania.

Color.—*Outside petal*—Outside surface—Lemon Yellow base to Martius Yellow, Plate IV, edged Rose Pink, Plate XII. Inside surface—Lemon Yellow base to Martius Yellow, Plate IV, edged Rose Pink, Plate XII. *Intermediate petal*—Outside surface—Lemon Yellow base to Martius Yellow, Plate IV, edged Rose Pink, Plate XII. Inside surface—Lemon Yellow base to Martius Yellow, Plate IV, edged Rose Pink, Plate XII. *Inner petal*—Outside surface—Lemon Yellow base to Martius Yellow, Plate IV, edged Rose Pink, Plate XII. Inside surface—Lemon Yellow base to Martius Yellow, Plate IV, edged Rose Pink, Plate XII.

This description was made from a rose that was open for three days outdoors, in November, 1941, at West Grove, Pennsylvania.

Color.—*Outside petal*—Outside surface—Lemon Yellow base to Martius Yellow, Plate IV, edged Rose Pink, Plate XII. Inside surface—Lemon Yellow base to Martius Yellow, Plate IV, edged Rose Pink, Plate XII. *Inside petal*—Outside surface—Lemon Yellow base to Martius Yellow, Plate IV, edged Rose Pink, Plate XII. Inside surface—Lemon Yellow base to Martius Yellow, Plate IV, edged Rose Pink, Plate XII.

General color effect.—Newly opened flower—Martius Yellow, Plate IV. Three days open—Martius Yellow, Plate IV.

Behavior.—Drop off cleanly; do not fade.

Flower longevity.—On bush in garden four to five days in November. Cut roses grown outdoors kept at living room temperatures four to six days in November.

Reproductive organs

Stamens: Many; arranged irregularly.

Filaments: Short and long; Nopal Red, Plate I; most with anthers.

Anthers: Medium size; Light Orange Yellow, Plate III; open at various times.

Pollen: Abundant; Capucine Yellow.

Pistils: Many.

Styles: Medium length; thin; bunched.

Stigma: Straw Yellow, Plate XVI.

Ovaries: All enclosed in calyx.

2 591

Hips: Short; pointed; with inconspicuous neck; pear-shaped; Bice Green, Plate XVII; smooth; walls thick, fleshy.

Sepals: Falling soon; moderately long; spear-shaped; recurved.

Seeds: Few; medium large.

Plant

Foliage:

Leaves.—Compound of five leaflets; normal; large; leathery; glossy.

Leaflets.—Ovoid with apex acute; base round; margin serrate.

Color.—*Mature*—Upper surface—Dark Varleys Green, Plate XVIII. Under surface—Light Elm Green, Plate XVII. *Young*—Upper surface—Roman Green, Plate XVI, veiled with Claret-Brown, Plate I. Under surface—Varleys Green, Plate XVIII, shaded Claret-Brown, Plate I.

Rachis.—Medium heavy; upper side, smooth, grooved; under side, sparsely thorny.

Stipules.—Medium long; medium wide; moderately long points, turning out at an angle of less than 45°, recurved toward the stem.

Disease.—Resistant to mildew and blackspot.

Growth:

Habit.—Upright; much branched.

Growth.—Vigorous.

Canes.—Moderately heavy.

Main stems.—Dull Cedar Green, Plate VI. *Thorns*—several; medium long; straight; hooked downward; with narrow base. *Prickles*—none. *Hairs*—none.

Branches.—Dull Cedar Green, Plate VI. *Thorns*—several; medium long; hooked downward; with narrow base. *Prickles*—none. *Hairs*—none.

New shoots.—Bright Victoria-Lake, Plate I. *Thorns*—many; medium long; hooked downward; with narrow base. *Prickles*—none. *Hairs*—none.

I claim:

A new and distinct variety of rose plant of the hybrid tea class, characterized as to novelty by its exceptionally vigorous growing habit and enduring quality of its foliage, size and perfection of form of the bloom, and their unusual blend of coloring, substantially as shown and described.

FRANCIS MEILLAND.

9

A Worldwide Patent System

A patent is enforceable only in the country that grants it. Your patent, for example, does not prevent someone from making your invention in Japan or selling it in England. However, most foreign countries do have patent laws, and you are eligible to file for protection under them.

There are several things to keep in mind when filing for a foreign patent. Most countries require that you pay fees on your patent after it has been granted, and in many countries these fees continue to increase throughout the life of your patent. So, unless you are making money on your invention, a foreign patent may not be a worthwhile investment. Also, patent laws vary greatly from country to country. Filing for a foreign patent is a very confusing business and will take a great deal of your time.

Fortunately, there have been moves toward a worldwide patent system, most recently the European Patent Convention (EPC) and the Patent Cooperation Treaty (PCT).

THE EPC

Under the guidelines of the EPC, you can obtain a patent in all member countries with a single application. The advantage, of course, is that you do not have to file a separate application in each country. The disadvantage is that if your application is successfully opposed, or if your patent is revoked, in one country, the same applies to all the other member countries. Members of the European Patent Convention are: the Federal Republic of Germany, Switzerland, the United Kingdom, France, Luxembourg, Sweden, Austria, the Netherlands, Liechtenstein, Belgium, and Italy.

THE PCT

The PCT is an agreement under which the filing of a single international application is, in effect, the filing of a national application in each country. The international application matures into a number of national applications that are processed in accordance with the patent laws of each country and, if successful, will result in the grant of national patents. Each country grants a patent on your invention separately. The PCT simply provides a standardized application format. When you file your PCT application, you select the member countries in which you want your patent to apply. You then have 20 months to pay the fees and furnish translations of your application to each country you select.

The countries that have signed the Patent Cooperation Treaty are: Finland, the Democratic People's Republic of Korea, Hungary, Australia, Liechtenstein, Norway, Romania, the Netherlands, Monaco, Austria, Denmark, Japan, Sweden, Luxembourg, Brazil, the Soviet Union, France, the United Kingdom, Switzerland, the Congo, the Federal Republic of Germany, the United States, Gabon, Togo, Chad, Cameroon, the Malagasy Republic (Madagascar), Malawi, Senegal, and the Central African Empire. Belgium and Italy have membership in the PCT pending, and other countries will join soon.

THE PCT-EPC APPLICATION

There are only a few areas in which the PCT, and the EPC, application requirements differ from the requirements for a U.S. application. PCT-EPC applications should be prepared on A4, 8 x 11, size paper (21 cm by 29.7 cm), there must be 1½ spaces between lines, the pages should be numbered at the top, and the title of your invention should appear at the beginning of the abstract and at the beginning of the description. The abstract should be on a separate sheet *after* the claims. You may prepare your drawings on the same size paper for use for U.S. applications, but keep in mind that the drawing paper will be cut down to A4 size. So, don't exceed the PCT margins or your drawing will be cropped.

A sample PCT application follows on pages 68–70.

Advantages of Using the PCT

- The filing of one application in the U.S. Patent and Trademark Office will be effective as a regular national filing in each country designated. This greatly simplifies the filing of applications for foreign patents since it is not necessary to initially pay fees in foreign currency or to know the various procedures and time limits for filing in each individual country. Record keeping should also be simplified.

- The English language will be used for filing and processing the international application up to at least the time when national processing begins.

- An application in the standardized format required for international applications will be accepted as an application for national processing by each designated country. The use of a standard application format may reduce some of the costs of foreign patent agents in foreign countries.

- Foreign patent agents are not required until procedures before the designated offices begin 20 months after the priority date.

- The U.S. applicant will receive a search report on the invention, prepared by the U.S. Patent and Trademark Office acting as an International Searching Authority. This report will permit the applicant to assess the potential of the invention and the value of continuing to seek patent protection in the various designated countries before having to pay national fees and prepare translations.

- The U.S. applicant will have at least 8 months' time in addition to the 12 months presently available under the Paris Convention—a total of 20 months from the priority date—to assess the potential of the invention and to evaluate the desirability of continuing to seek patent protection in the various designated countries before paying national fees and furnishing translations.

- The PCT may be an attractive route for a U.S. applicant to file an application under the European Patent Convention (EPC). By using the PCT route to the EPC, the applicant may delay the payment of all EPC fees until 21 months after the filing of the first application on the invention.

PCT Fees

Transmittal fee	**$35**	Designation fees	
Search fee	**$300**	for each national patent	**$45**
Supplemental Search fee	**$200 per invention**	for each regional patent	**$45**

(The following is to be filled in by the receiving Office)
INTERNATIONAL APPLICATION No:

INTERNATIONAL FILING DATE:

(Stamp)
Name of receiving Office and "PCT International Application"

Applicant's or Agent's File Reference [9]
(indicated by applicant if desired).

INTERNATIONAL APPLICATION UNDER THE PATENT COOPERATION TREATY

REQUEST

THE UNDERSIGNED REQUESTS THAT THE PRESENT INTERNATIONAL APPLICATION BE PROCESSED ACCORDING TO THE PATENT COOPERATION TREATY

I. TITLE OF INVENTION [1]

II. APPLICANT [2] Additional information is contained in supplemental box. ☐

Name [3, 5]

Address [4, 5] (including postal code and country)

Nationality [5, 6] (country)	Residence [5, 7] (country)

Telephone number (if any) [4]	Telegraphic address (if any) [4, 5]	Teleprinter address (if any) [4, 5]

III. INVENTOR [8] (Applicant is also the inventor ☐) Additional information is contained in supplemental box. ☐

Name [3, 5]

Address [4, 5] (including postal code and country)

IV. AGENT OR COMMON REPRESENTATIVE (IF ANY) [9] Additional information is contained in supplemental box. ☐

A. ☐ Applicant hereby appoints the following named agent or common representative to act on his behalf before the competent International Authorities. [9]

B. ☐ Applicant has appointed the following named agent or common representative in accompanying separate power of attorney. [9]

Name [3, 5]

Address [4, 5] (including postal code and country).

Telephone number (if any) [4]	Telegraphic address (if any) [4, 5]	Teleprinter address (if any) [4, 5]

V. DESIGNATION OF STATES [10] (and possible indication of wish to obtain regional patents) [11] (and possible choice of certain kinds of protection) [12] Additional information is contained in supplemental box. ☐

RO use

VI. PRIORITY CLAIM (IF ANY) [13] Additional information is contained in supplemental box. ☐

The priority of an earlier application is claimed (indicate following data):

Country (If the earlier application is regional or international application, indicate those countries for which it was filed).	Filing Date [14]
	Application Number [15]
	If a regional or international application, indicate the national Office or intergovernmental organization with which it was filed.

VII. PARENT APPLICATION OR GRANT (IF ANY) [16] Additional information is contained in supplemental box. ☐

Designated State	Type of Treatment Desired	Number and Title of the Parent Application or Grant	Filing Date of the Parent Application or Grant [14]

VIII. EARLIER INTERNATIONAL OR INTERNATIONAL-TYPE SEARCH (IF ANY) [17] Additional information is contained in supplemental box. ☐

An earlier ☐ international or ☐ international-type search has been requested on the following application

Receiving Office/Country	(International) Application No.	(International) Filing Date [14]

Date of Request for the Search where the Earlier Search was an International-Type Search [14]	Number given by the International Searching Authority to the Request for Search where the Earlier Search was an International-Type Search

IX. DIFFERENT APPLICANTS FOR DIFFERENT (GROUPS OF) DESIGNATED STATES (WHERE APPLICABLE) [18]

Additional information is contained in supplemental box. ☐

Designated States	Name of Applicant

X. DIFFERENT INVENTORS FOR DIFFERENT (GROUPS OF) DESIGNATED STATES (WHERE APPLICABLE) [19]

Additional information is contained in supplemental box. ☐

Designated States	Name of Inventor

Form PCT/RO/101 (second sheet) (April 1978) (U.S. Version) See notes on accompanying sheet

SUPPLEMENTAL BOX... USE THIS BOX IF ANY OF THE BOXES IS NOT LARGE ENOUGH TO CONTAIN INFORMATION TO BE FURNISHED. INDICATE THE BOXES CONTINUED IN THIS BOX BY THEIR (ROMAN) NUMERALS AND TITLE (e.g.: "II. APPLICANT (CONTINUED)")

XI. **SIGNATURE OF APPLICANT** [20]

XII. **CHECK LIST** (To be filled in by the Applicant) [21]

A. This international application contains the following number of sheets:

1. request .... sheets
2. description .... sheets
3. claims .... sheets
4. abstract .... sheets
5. drawings .... sheets

Total sheets

C. Figure number .... of the drawings (if any) is suggested to accompany the abstract for publication.

D. Drawings (To be filled in by the receiving Office)
☐ No Drawings [22]

B. This international application as filed is accompanied by the items checked below:

1. ☐ separate signed power of attorney
2. ☐ priority document
3. ☐ fee calculation sheet (PCT/RO/101 (Annex))
4. ☐ check for the payment of fees
5. ☐ international search report
6. ☐ international-type search report
7. ☐ document in evidence of fact that applicant is successor in title of inventor
8. ☐ other document (specify)

(The following is to be filled in by the receiving Office)

1. Date of actual receipt of the purported international application:
2. Corrected date of actual receipt due to later but timely received papers or drawings completing the purported international application:
3. Date of timely receipt of the required corrections under Article 11 of the PCT:

(The following is to be filled in by the International Bureau)

Date of receipt of the record copy:

Form PCT/RO/101 (last sheet) (April 1978) (U.S. Version)

See notes on accompanying sheet

Appendix One

Patents Price List

The following prices are subject to change. To verify prices and other information, contact the Patent and Trademark Office, Washington, D.C. 20231.

Filing fee. On filing each application for an original patent, except in design cases **$65**

In addition:

On filing or on presentation at any other time, for each claims in independent form which is in excess of one **$10**

For each claim (whether independent or dependent) which is in excess of 10 **$2**

Errors in payment of the additional fees may be rectified in accordance with regulations of the Commissioner.

Issue fee. For issuing each original or reissue patent, except in design cases **$100**

In addition:

For each page (or portion thereof) of specification as printed **$10**

For each sheet of drawing **$2**

In design cases:

On filing each design application **$20**

On issuing each design patent:

For 3 years and 6 months **$10**

For 7 years **$20**

For 14 years **$30**

Reissues. On filing each application for the reissue of patent **$65**

In addition:

On filing or on presentation at any other time, for each claim in independent form which is in excess of the number of independent claims of the original patent **$10**

For each claim (whether independent or dependent) which is in excess of ten and also in excess of the number of claims of the original patent **$2**

Errors in payment of the additional fees may be rectified in accordance with regulations of the Commissioner.

On filing each disclaimer **$15**

On filing each petition for the revival of an abandoned application for patent **$15**

On filing each petition for the delayed payment of the issue fee **$15**

On appeal for the first time from the examiner to the Board of Appeals **$50**

On filing a brief in support of the appeal **$50**

For certification of copies of records, etc., in any case, in addition to the cost of copy certified **$1**
For certificate of correction of applicant's mistake **$15**
For uncertified copies of the specifications and accompanying drawings of patents, except design patents **.50**
For uncertified copies of design patents **.20**
For recording every assignment, agreement, or other paper relating to the property in a patent or application **$20**
For additional item, where the document relates to more than one patent or application **$3**
For typewritten copies of records, for each page produced (double-spaced) or fraction thereof **$1.50**
For photocopies or other reproduction of records, drawings or printed material, per page of material copied **.30**
For abstracts of title to each patent or application:
For the search, one hour or less, and certificate **$3**
Each additional hour or fraction thereof **$1.50**
For each brief from the digest of assignments, of 200 words or less **$1**
Each additional 100 words or fraction thereof **.10**
For translations from foreign languages into English, made only of references cited in applications or of papers filed in the Patent and Trademark Office insofar as facilities may be available:
Written translations, for every 100 words of the original language, or fraction thereof **$5**
Oral translations (dictation or assistance), for each one-half hour or fraction thereof that service is rendered **$4**
For making patent drawings, when facilities are available, the cost of making the same, minimum charge per sheet **$25**
For correcting drawings, the cost of making the correction, minimum charge **$3**
For the mounting of unmounted drawings and photoprints received with patent applications, provided they are of approved permanency **$2**
Lists of U.S. Patents:
- All patents in a subclass, per sheet (containing 100 patent numbers or less) **.50**
- Minimum charge per order **$1**
- Patents in a subclass limited by date or patent number, per sheet (containing 50 numbers or less) **.50**
- Minimum charge per order **$1**

Search of Patent and Trademark Office records for purposes not otherwise specified in this section, per one-half hour of search or fraction thereof **$3**
For special service to expedite furnishing items or services ahead of regular order:
On orders for copies of U.S. patents and trademark registrations, in addition to the charge for the copies, for each copy ordered **.50**

On all other orders or requests for which special service facilities are available, in addition to the regular charge, a special service charge equal to the amount of regular charge; minimum special service charge per order or request **$1**
For air mail delivery:
On 'special service' orders to destinations to which U.S. domestic air mail postage rates apply, no additional charge.
On regular service orders to any destination and "special service" orders to destination other than those specified in the preceding subparagraph, an additional charge equal to the amount of air mail postage. (Available only when the ordering party has, with the Patent and Trademark Office, a deposit account.)
For items and services, that the Commissioner finds may be supplied, for which fees are not specified by statute or by this section, such charge as may be determined by the Commissioner with respect to each such item or service.
International application filing and processing fees.

The following fees and charges are established by the Patent and Trademark Office under the authority of 35 U.S.C. 376:

A transmittal fee (see 35 U.S.C. 361(d) and PCT Rule 14) **$35**

A search fee (see 35 U.S.C. 361(d) and PCT Rule 16) **$300**

A supplemental search fee when required (see PCT Art. 17(3) (a) and PCT Rule 40.2)—per additional invention **$200**

The national fee, that is, the amount set forth as the filing fee under 35 U.S.C. 41(a) (1).

A special fee when required (see 35 U.S.C. 372(c))—per claim **$10**

The basic fee and designation fee portions of the international fee shall be as prescribed in PCT Rule 15.

Legislation has recently been passed to enable the PTO to raise its fees every three years until it recovers half the cost of examining patent applications and issuing patents. A 60-day notice in the Federal Register is required before new fees go into effect.

Briefly, the filing and issue fees will equal 25% of the cost. Maintenance fees, at 3½-, 7½-, and 11-year intervals after your patent has issued, will equal the other 25%. For design applications, the filing and issue fees will equal 50% and there will be no maintenance fees.

Since credit will be given only when a full fee is paid, you should plan ahead and inquire of the PTO what the current fee is, particularly the filing fee,so that you will receive the earliest filing data possible.

Appendix Two

Libraries with Patent Collections

Alabama
Birmingham Public Library
205-254-2555
California
Los Angeles Public Library
213-626-7555 Ext. 274
Sacramento: California State Library
916-322-4572
Sunnyvale Patent Library*
408-738-5580
Colorado
Denver Public Library
303-573-5152 Ext. 223
Delaware
University of Delaware
302-738-2238
Georgia
Atlanta: Price Gilbert Memorial Library, Georgia Institute of Technology
404-894-4519
Illinois
Chicago Public Library
312-269-2814
Massachusetts
Boston Public Library
617-536-5400 Ext. 265
Michigan
Detroit Public Library
313-833-1458
Minnesota
Minneapolis Public Library and Information Center
612-372-6552

* Collection organized by subject matter.

Missouri
Kansas City: Linda Hall Library
816-363-4600
St. Louis Public Library
314-241-2288 Ext. 214
Nebraska
Lincoln: University of Nebraska-Lincoln, Love Library
404-472-3411
New Hampshire
Durham: University of New Hampshire Library
603-862-1777
New Jersey
Newark Public Library
201-733-7740
New York
Albany: New York State Library
518-474-5125
Buffalo and Erie County Public Library
716-856-7525 Ext. 267
New York Public Library (The Research Libraries)
212-790-6291
North Carolina
Raleigh: D. H. Hill Library, N.C. State University
919-737-3280
Ohio
Public Library of Cincinnati & Hamilton County
513-369-6936
Cleveland Public Library
216-623-2932
Columbus: Ohio State University Libraries
614-422-6286
Toledo/Lucas County Public Library
419-255-7055 Ext. 212

Oklahoma
Stillwater: Oklahoma State University Library
405-624-6546
Pennsylvania
Philadelphia: Franklin Institute Library
215-448-1224; Call between noon and 5 P.M.
Pittsburgh: Carnegie Library of Pittsburgh
412-622-3138
University Park: Pattee Library, Pennsylvania State University Libraries
814-865-4861
Rhode Island
Providence Public Library
401-521-7722 Ext. 224
Tennessee
Memphis & Shelby County Public Library and Information Center
901-528-2957
Texas
Dallas Public Library
214-748-9071
Houston. The Fondren Library, Rice University
713-527-8101 Ext. 2587
Washington
Seattle: Engineering Library, University of Washington
206-543-0740
Wisconsin
Madison: Kurt F. Wendt Engineering Library, University of Wisconsin
608-262-6845
Milwaukee Public Library
414-278-3043

Appendix Three

Patents: A Historic View

Telephones, diesel engines, Polaroid cameras, and thousands of other modern "conveniences" were first introduced as patent applications. Today, these and four million other U.S. patents, six million foreign patents, and a great amount of technical information are stored in the U.S. Patent Office in Washington, D.C.

For 50 cents each, the Office will supply you with copies of these patents. Write to the U.S. Patent and Trademark Office, Washington, D.C. 20231. Be sure to include the patent number, which you can obtain from a library that has a patent collection (see the list on pages 74–75), or from the Patent Office.

Here is a sampling of the patents on file.

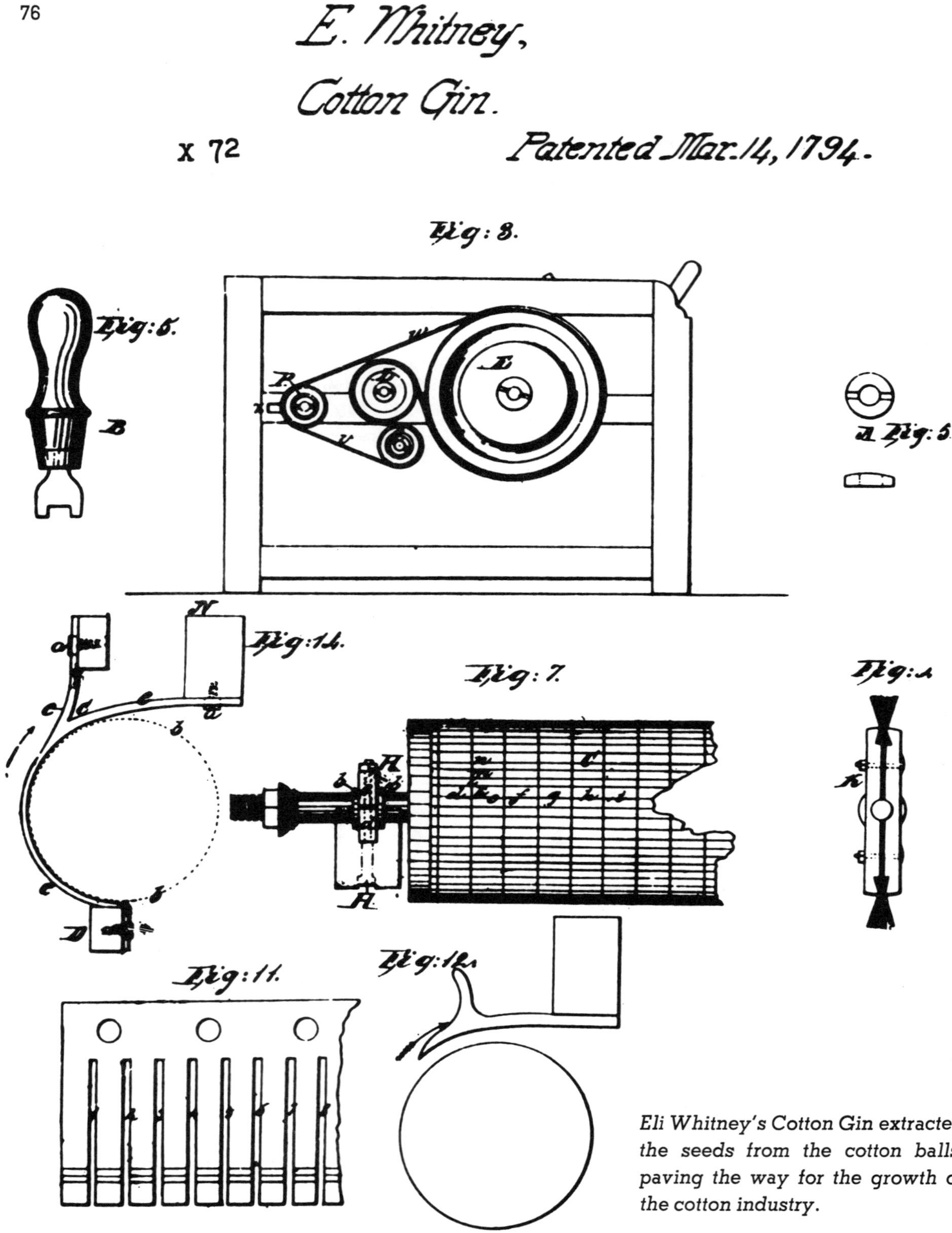

Eli Whitney's Cotton Gin extracted the seeds from the cotton balls, paving the way for the growth of the cotton industry.

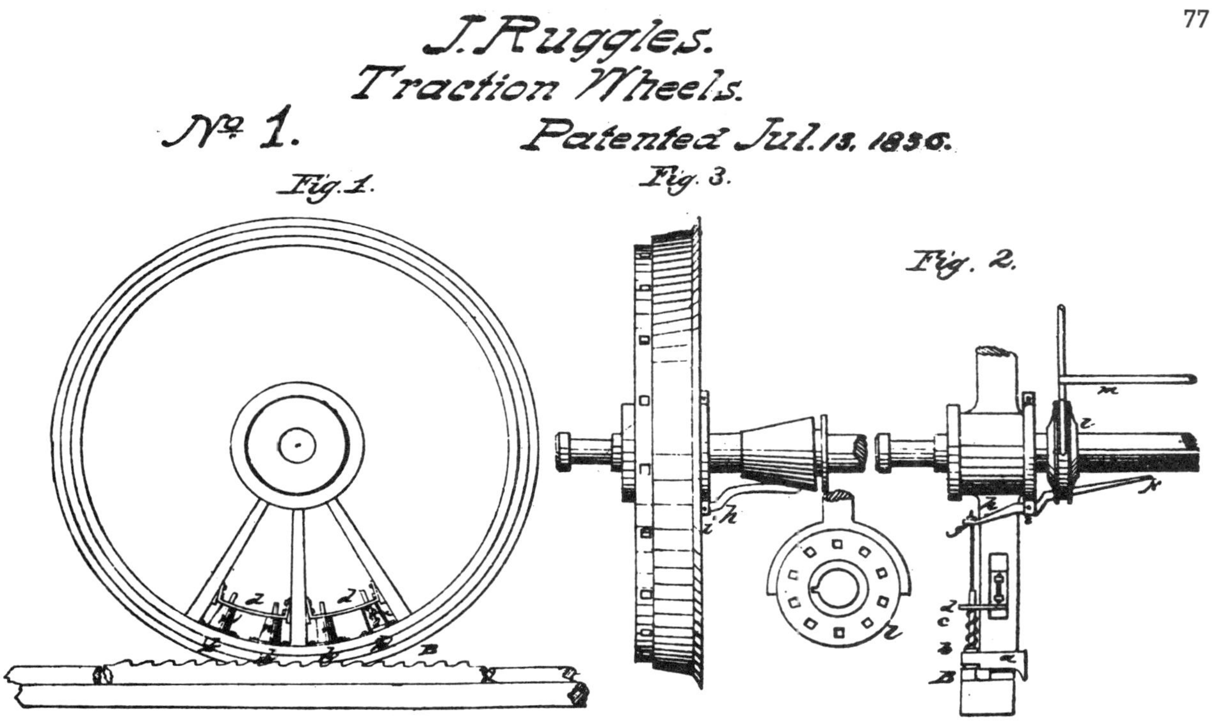

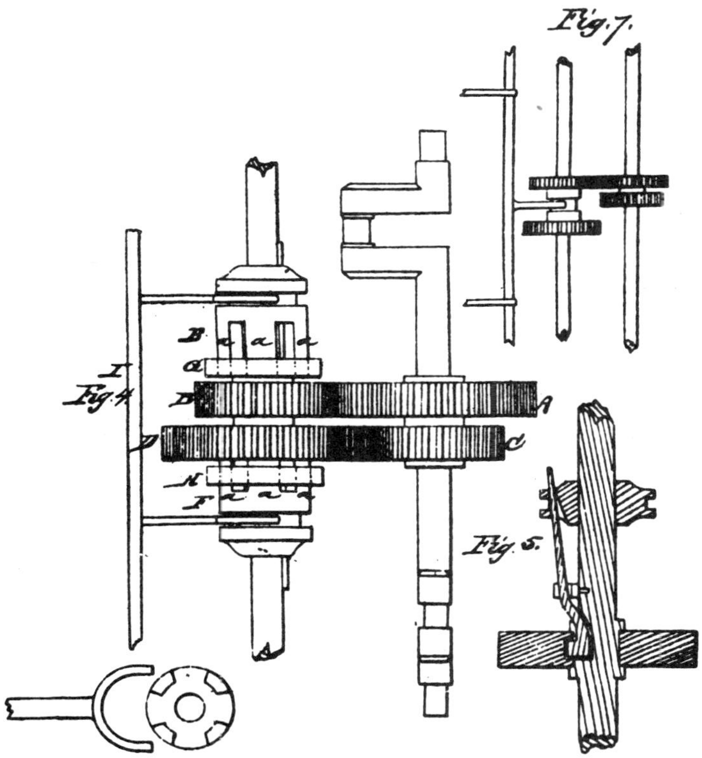

This was the first patent issued under our present patent system after the burning of the Patent Office during the War of 1812. The wheels have pins that catch in the notches on the rails to prevent slipping on hills.

S. COLT.

Revolving Gun.

Patented Feb. 25, 1836.

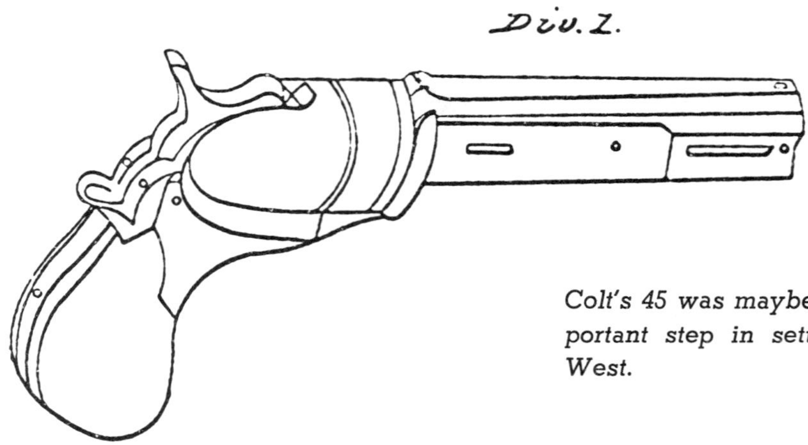

Colt's 45 was maybe the most important step in settling the Old West.

S. F. B. MORSE.

Telegraph Signs.

No. 1,647. Patented June 20, 1840

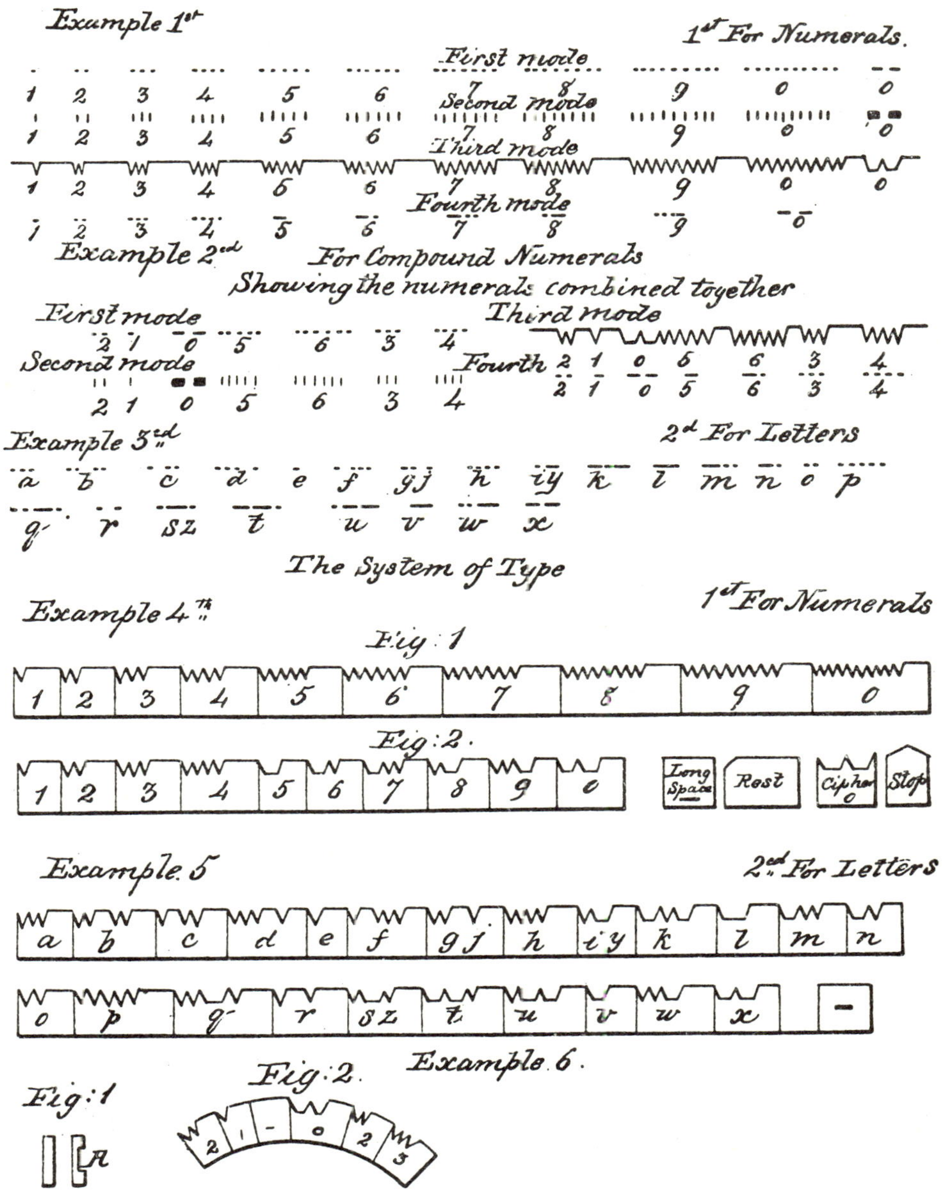

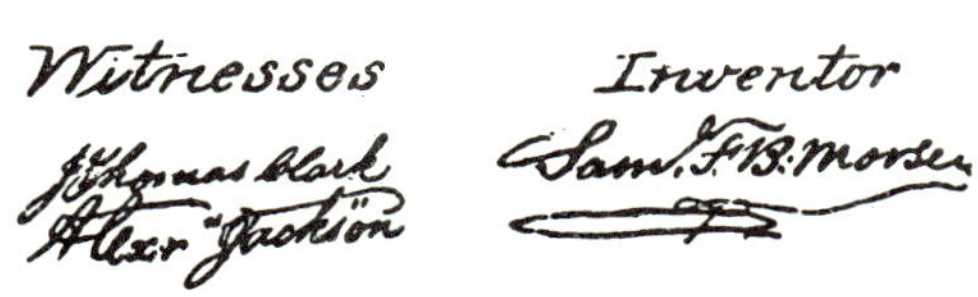

Morse's Telegraph revolutionized communications. The first lines were between Baltimore and Washington, and the first message was "What hath God wrought!"

S. Scotton,

Railroad Alarm.

No. 54,783. Patented May 15, 1866.

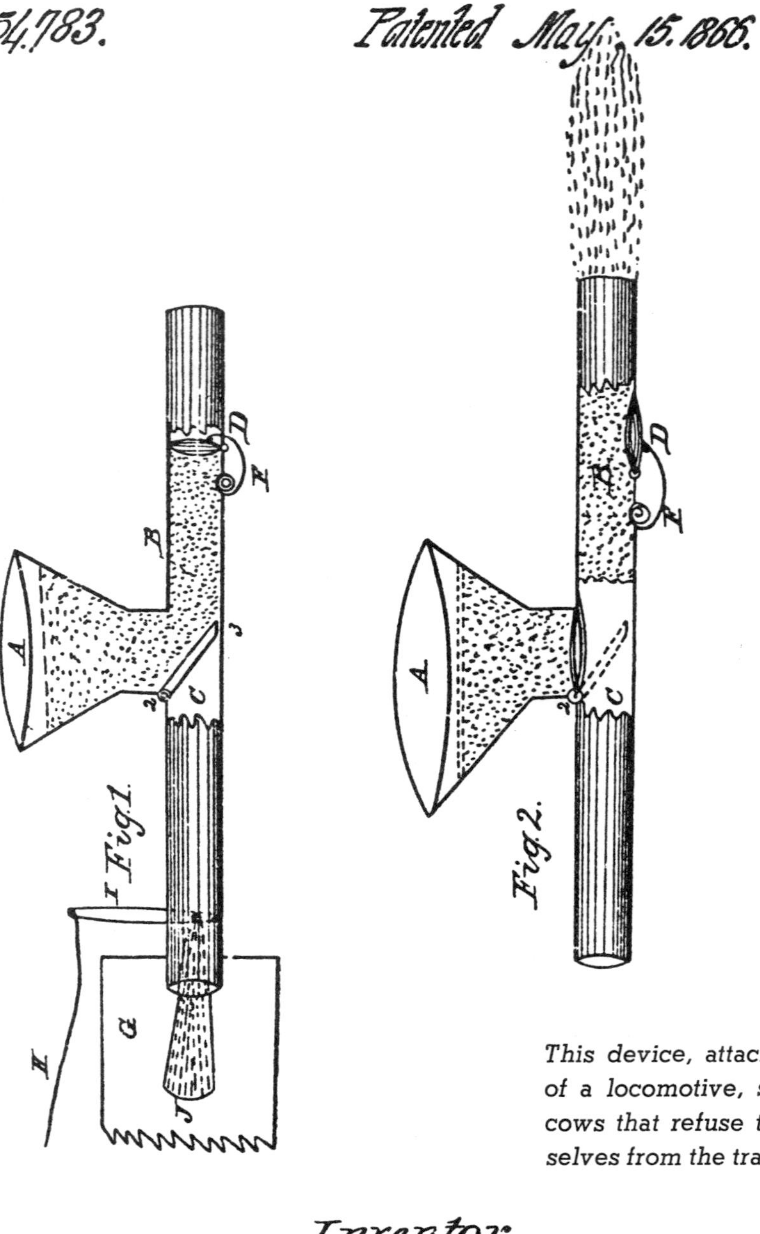

This device, attached to the front of a locomotive, shoots gravel at cows that refuse to remove themselves from the track.

Witnesses:
Adela L Scotton
Mary H Buchanan

Inventor:
Stephen Scotton

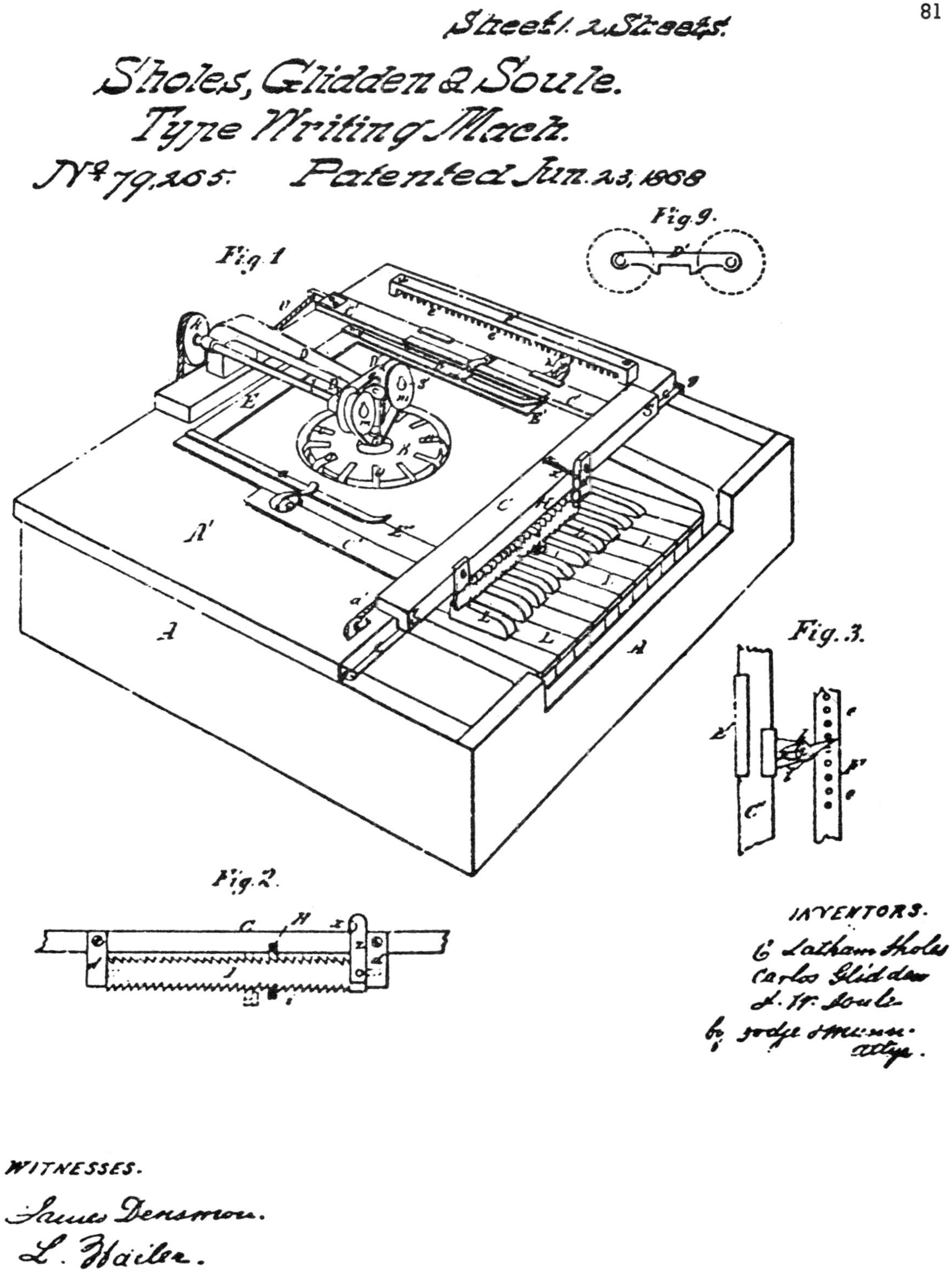

The modern typewriter is born.

C. Singer,

Rocking Chair.

No. 92,379. Patented July 6. 1869.

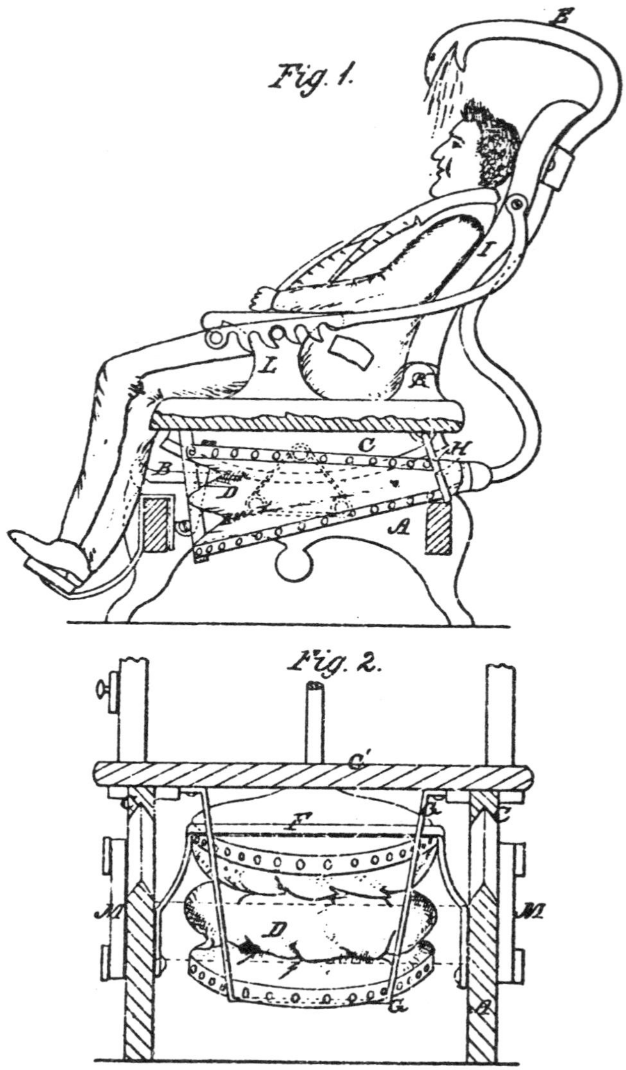

Witnesses,
O. Hinchman
Jno. K. Brooks

Inventor.
C. Singer
per Munn & Co
attys

The rocking motion sends a jet of cool air over the rocker's face.

(38.)

SAMUEL L. CLEMENS.

Improvement in Adjustable and Detachable Straps for Garments.

No. 121,992. Patented Dec. 19, 1871.

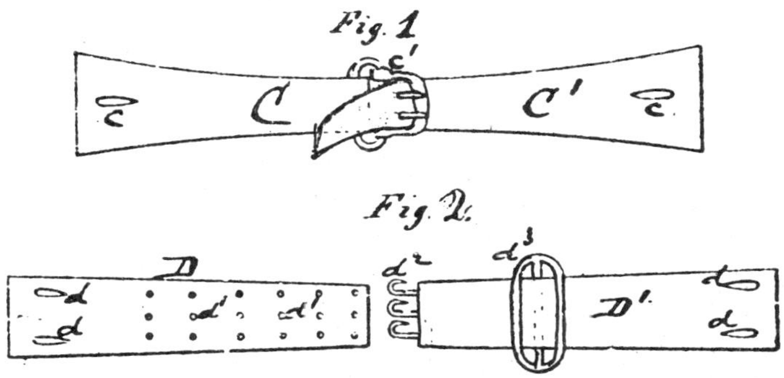

Witnesses:

Inventor

Attorneys.

Samuel Clemens did more than just write books; here's his idea for a vest snap.

S. L. CLEMENS.

Scrap-Books.

No. 140,245. Patented June 24, 1873.

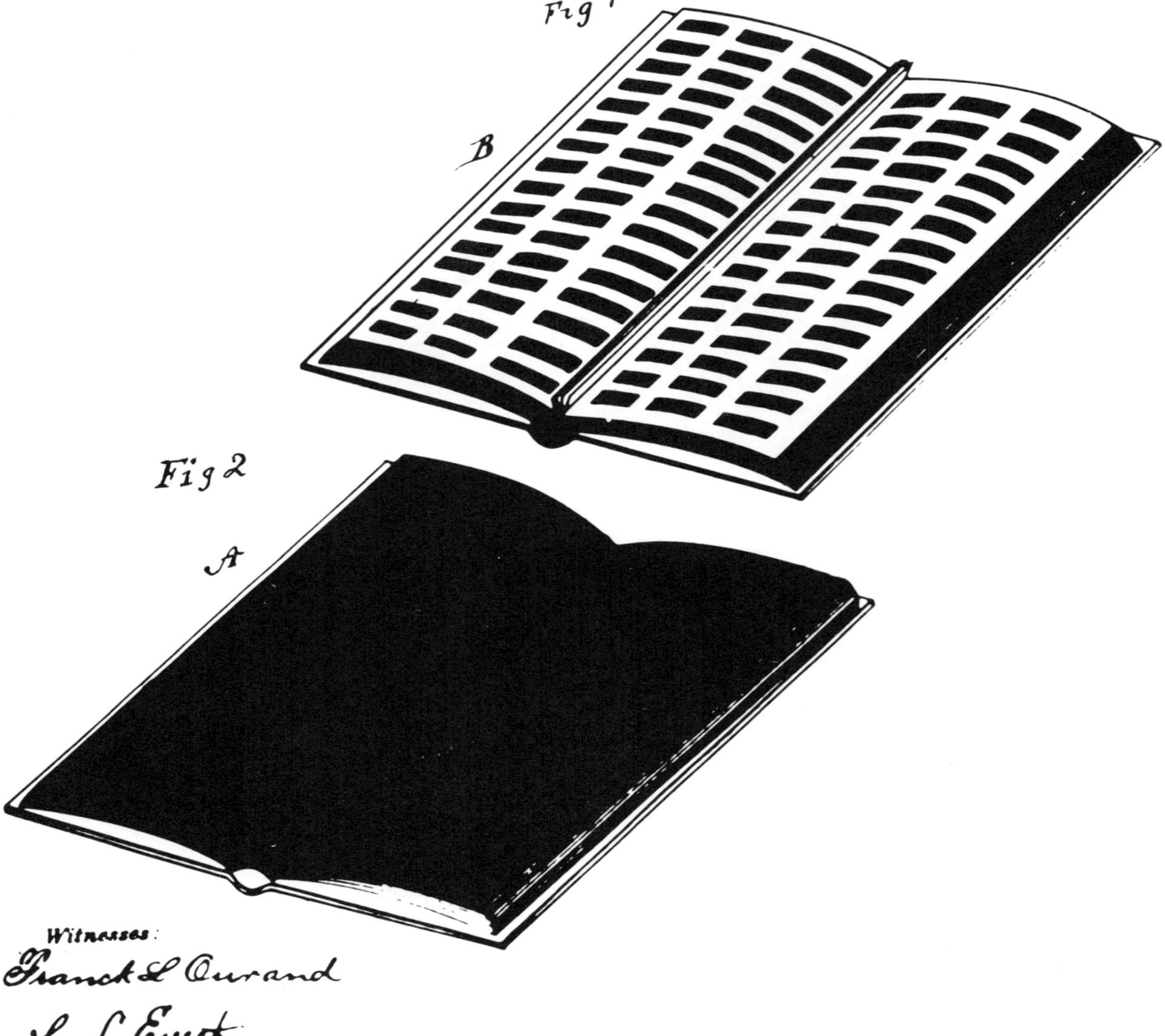

Witnesses:

Franck L. Ourand

C. L. Evert

Inventor

Samuel L. Clemens

per [illegible]

Attorney

Another Clemens' invention, a scrapbook. He applied glue to the pages in advance, then moistened them later. This way, he could paste in pictures and clippings without making a mess.

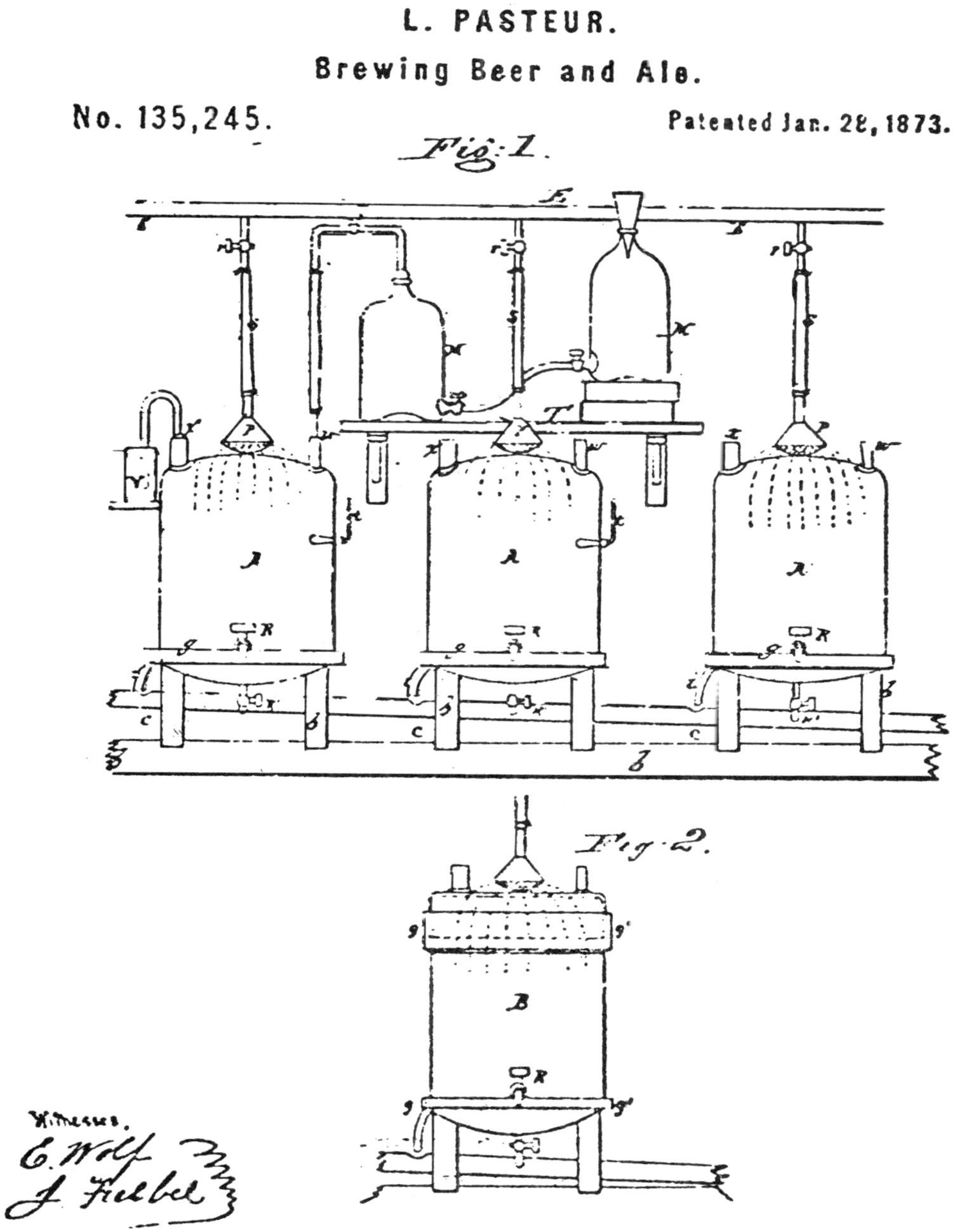

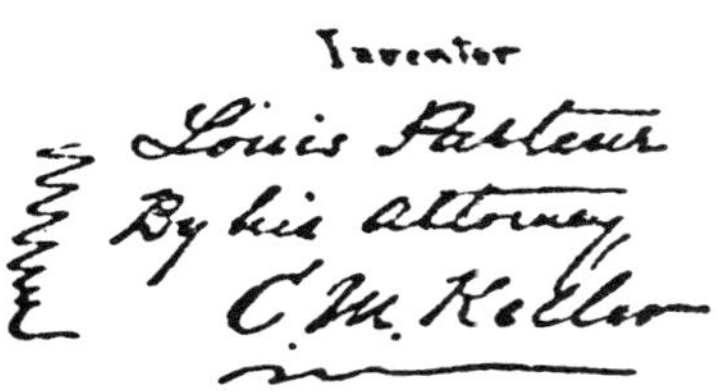

Louis Pasteur applied the principles of pasteurization to beer and ale.

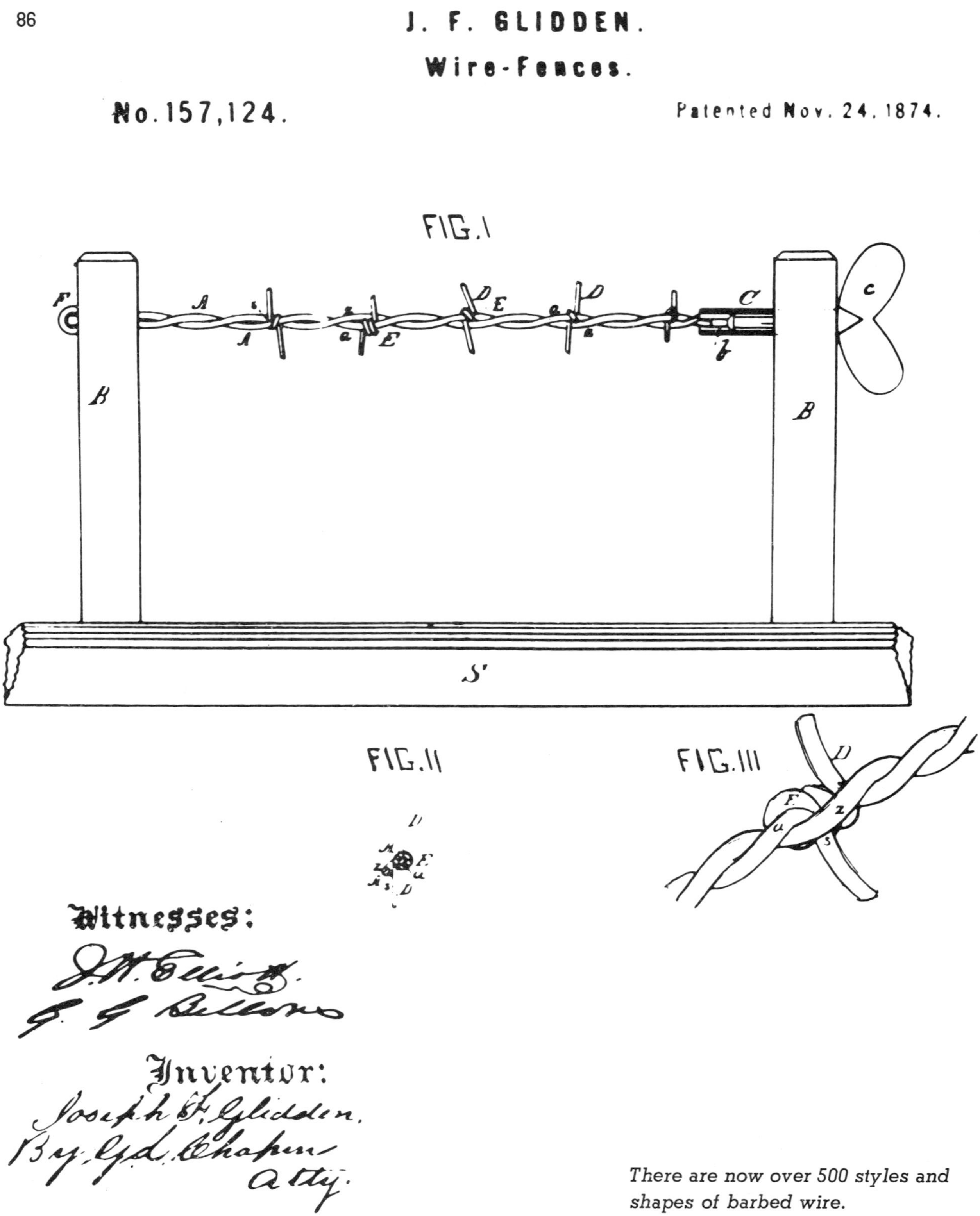

There are now over 500 styles and shapes of barbed wire.

T A EDISON.
Phonograph or Speaking Machine

No. 200,521. **Patented Feb. 19, 1878.**

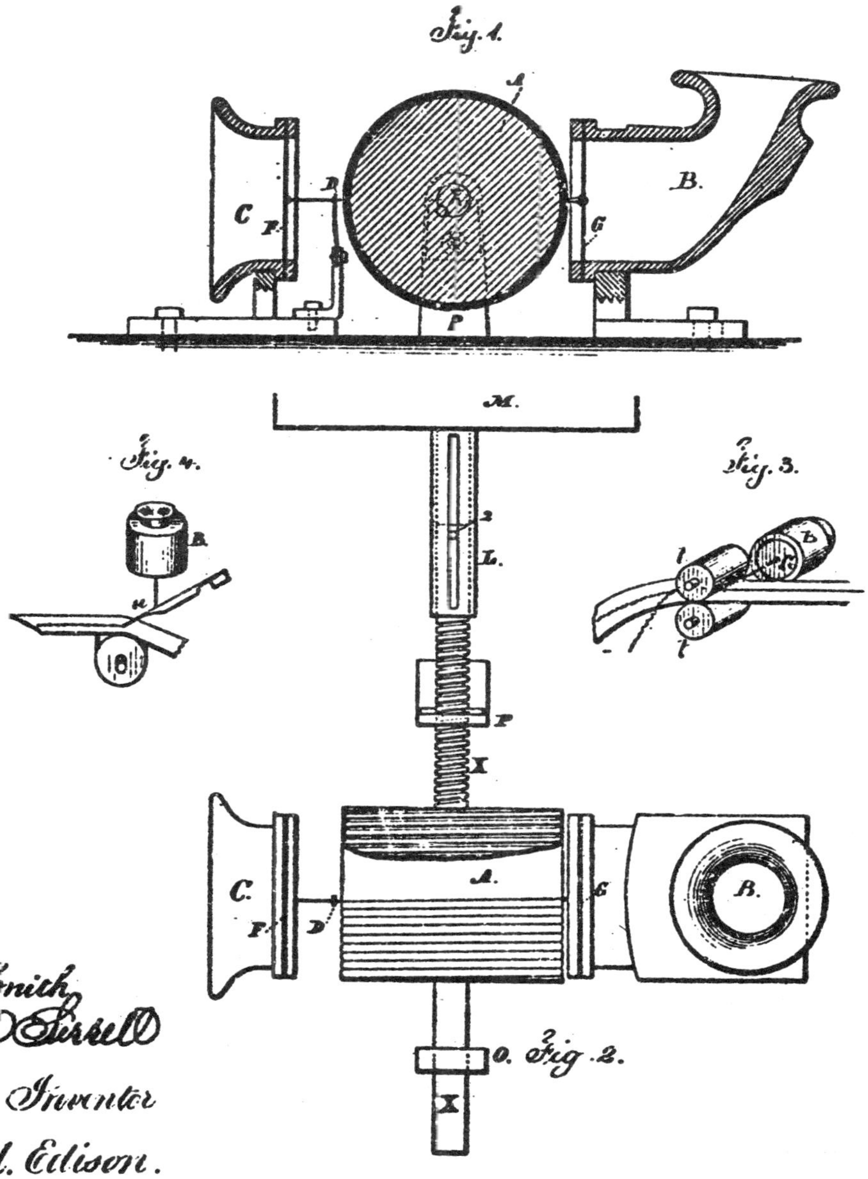

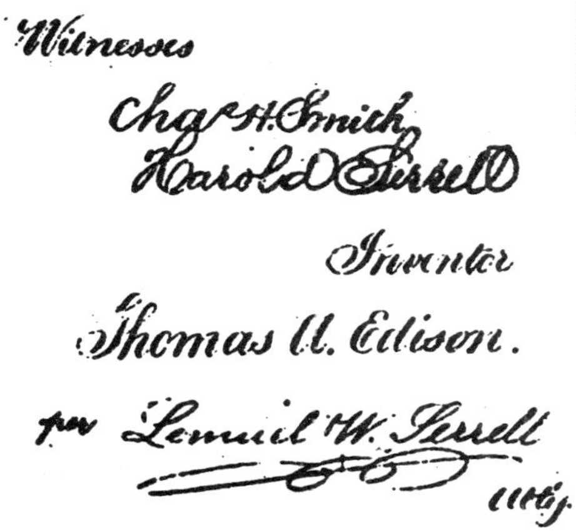

The phonograph was Edison's favorite of his 1,093 inventions. The public loved it, too, and hailed the young inventor as a "magician."

B. B. OPPENHEIMER.
Fire-Escape.

No. 221,855. **Patented Nov. 18, 1879.**

WITNESSES:

Henry N. Miller
C. Sedgwick

INVENTOR:

B. B. Oppenheimer

BY Munn & Co

ATTORNEYS

Small wonder this fire escape didn't catch on. Consisting of a parachute and padded shoes, it is not recommended for use above the second floor.

T. A. EDISON.
Electric-Lamp.

No. 223,898. **Patented Jan. 27, 1880.**

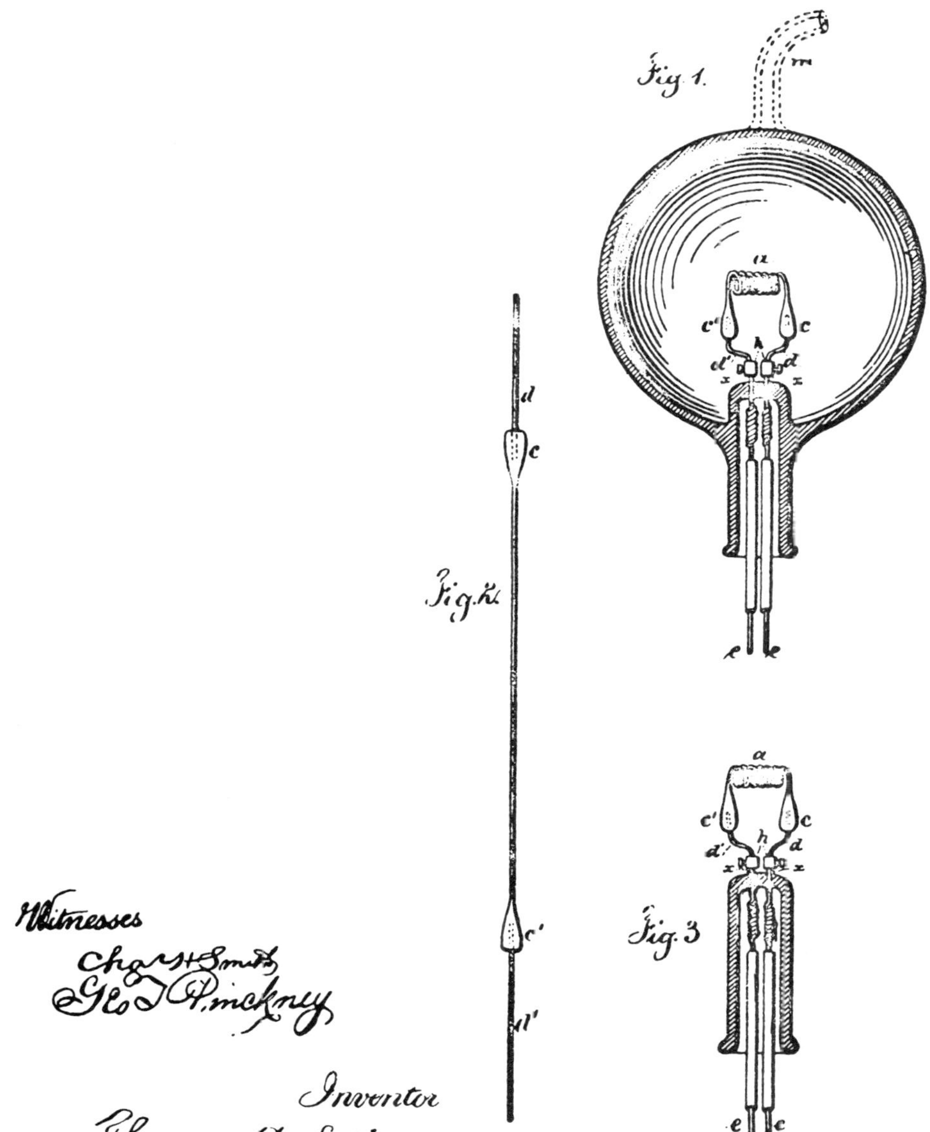

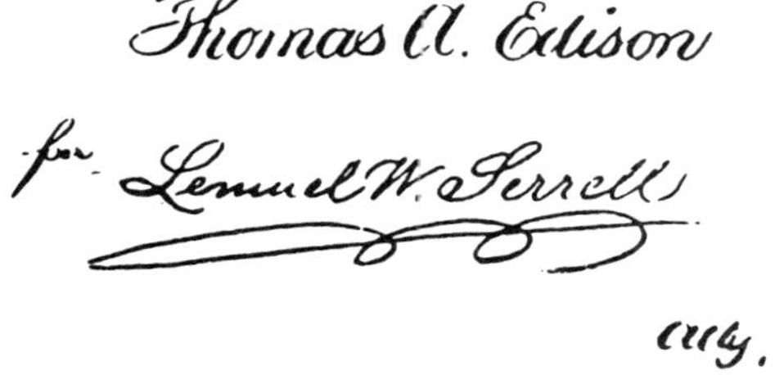

Edison's light has been compared to the wheel in its effect on civilization. It consists of a carbon filament sealed in an evacuated glass globe, and is bright, durable, and inexpensive to manufacture.

G. EASTMAN.

Method and Apparatus for Coating Plates for use in Photography.

No. 226,503. **Patented April 13, 1880.**

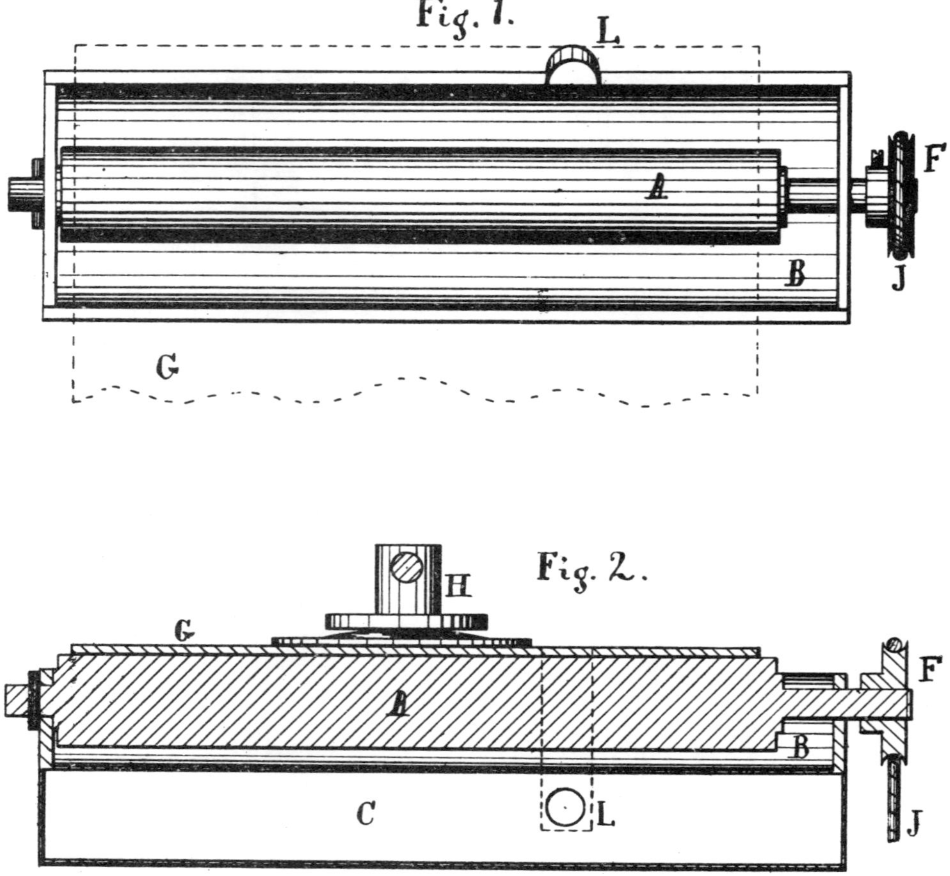

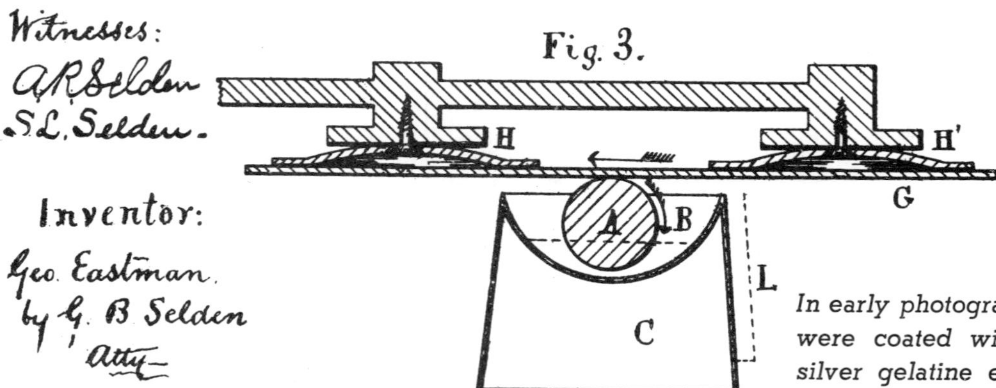

In early photography, glass plates were coated with a bromide-of-silver gelatine emulsion. George Eastman made the process easier with his 1,880 invention.

(No Model.)

G. H. KIRK.

CANDLE.

No. 276,602. Patented May 1, 1883.

FIG.1.

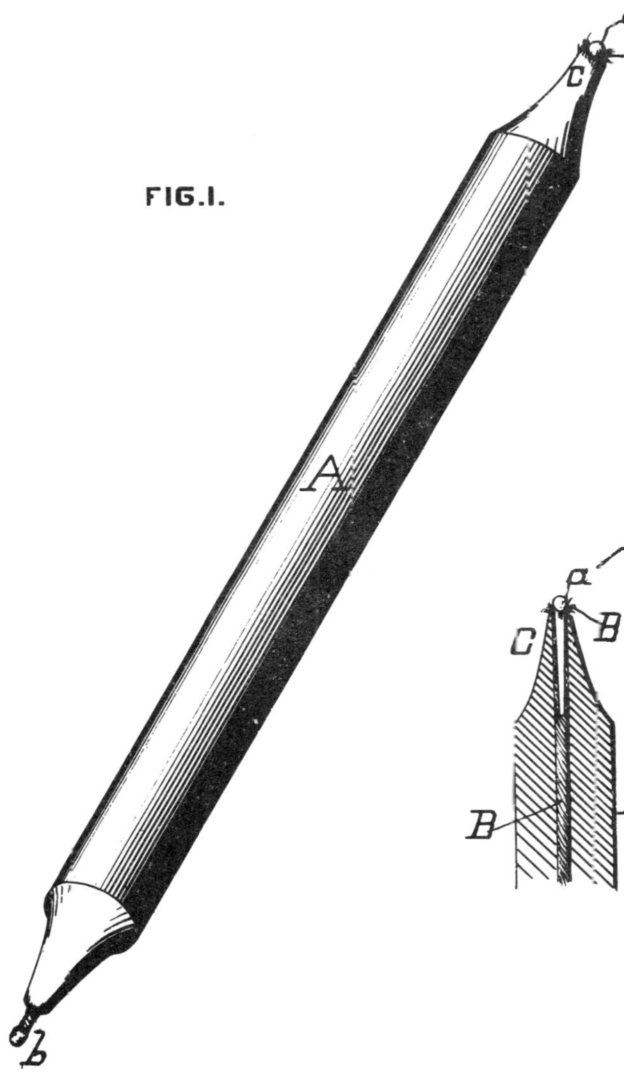

FIG.2.

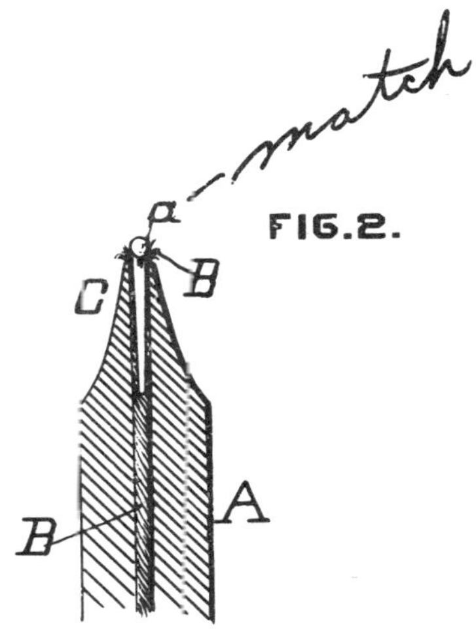

WITNESSES:

Joseph Enew

B. F. Timmons

INVENTOR

George H. Kirk

By Francis D. Pastorius

Attorney

A matchlike wick permits the user to light this candle by friction.

(No Model.)

LA FAYETTE W. PAGE.

ATTACHMENT FOR LOCOMOTIVES.

No. 292,504. Patented Jan. 29, 1884.

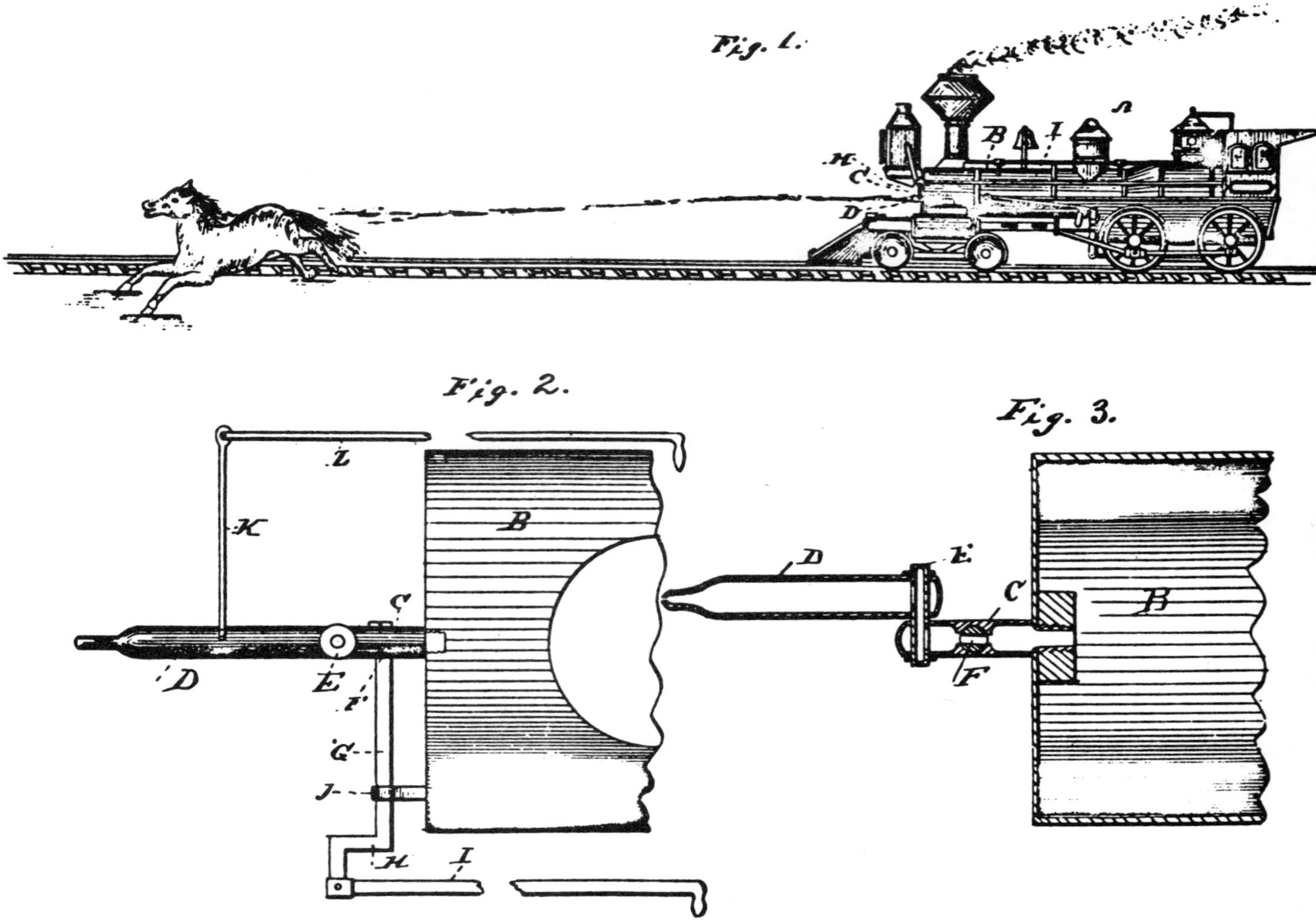

L. W. Page,
INVENTOR
by A. Snow & Co
Attorneys.

WITNESSES
W. E. Bowen
Chas. L. Burr

Stubborn animals could hold up a train for hours. This device shoots a stream of hot water from the locomotive's boiler at the beast.

(No Model.)

T. S. BRADY.

CHIN REST FOR TOBACCO PIPES.

No. 353,197. Patented Nov. 23, 1886.

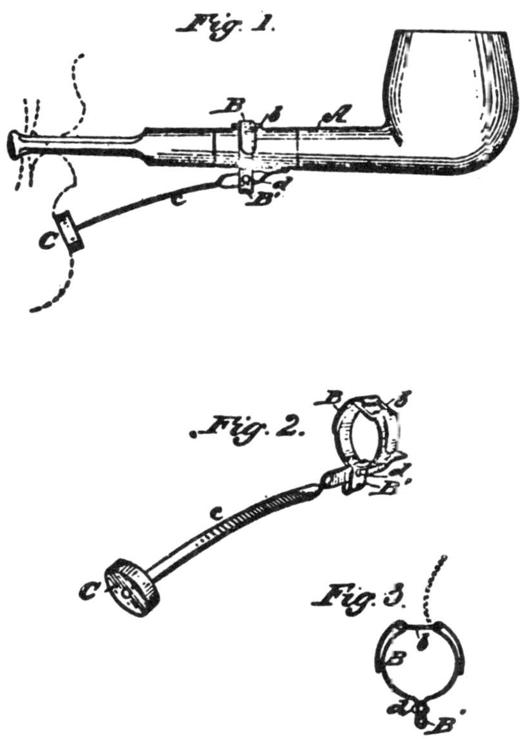

WITNESSES:

Benj. S. Van Wyck

INVENTOR
Thomas S. Brady
BY
Theodore Ritter
ATTORNEY

A chin rest for lazy pipe smokers.

(No Model.)

H. M. SMALL.

HAMMOCK.

No. 400,131. Patented Mar. 26, 1889.

Fig. 1.

Fig. 2.

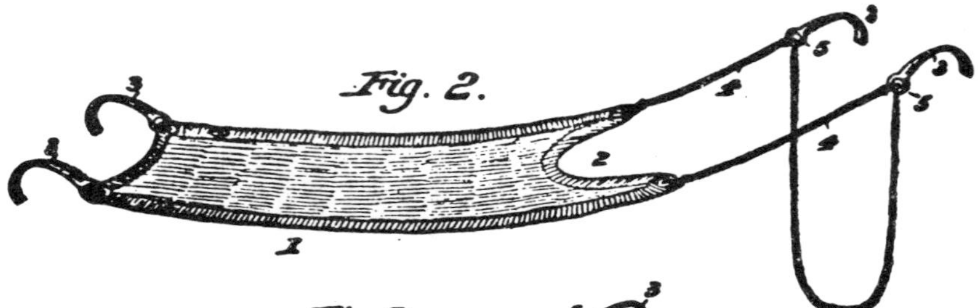

Fig. 3.

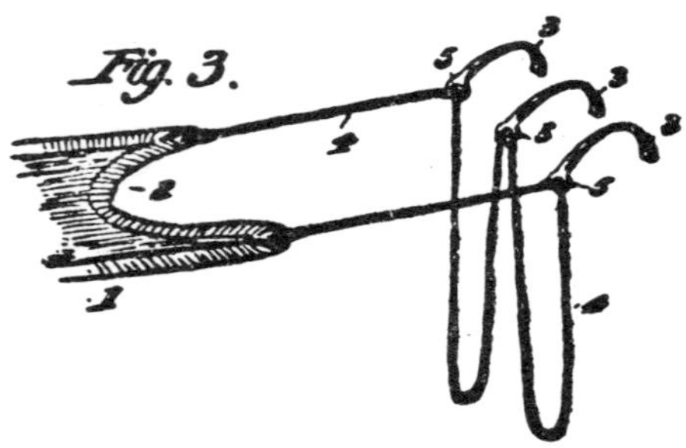

WITNESSES:

J. H. Clark.
E. Mc Clark.

INVENTOR:

H. M. Small

BY Munn & Co

ATTORNEYS.

When slung between train seats, this hammock serves as a comfortable(?) bed.

(No Model.)

C. W. ROBERTSON.

CHEWING GUM LOCKET.

No. 395,515. Patented Jan. 1, 1889.

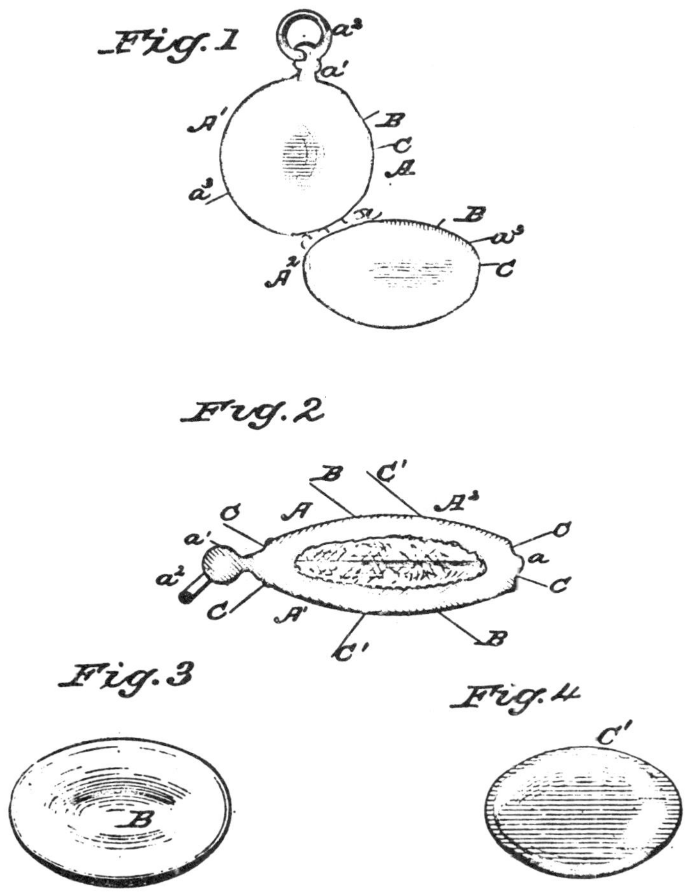

INVENTOR:

WITNESSES:

Fred G. Dieterich
Solon C. Kemon

C. W. Robertson
BY Munn & Co
ATTORNEYS.

This sanitary depository for chewing gum has an anticorrosive lining.

(No Model.)

A. SUEUR.

MUSICAL DECANTER.

No. 465,795. Patented Dec. 22, 1891.

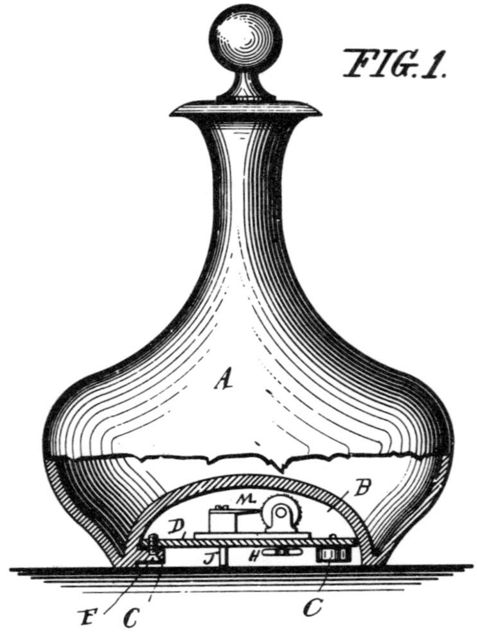

FIG. 1.

FIG. 2

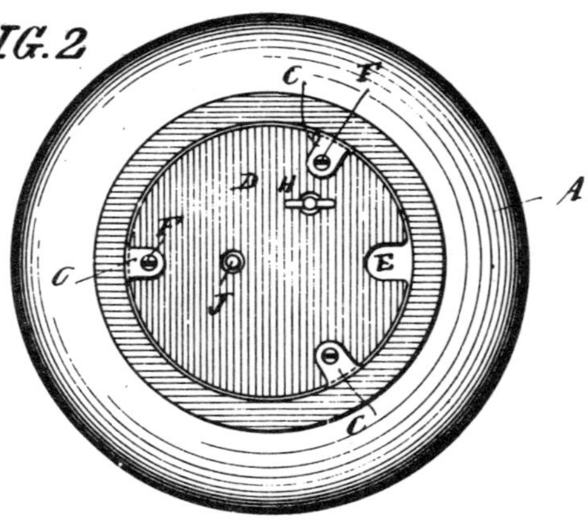

FIG. 3.

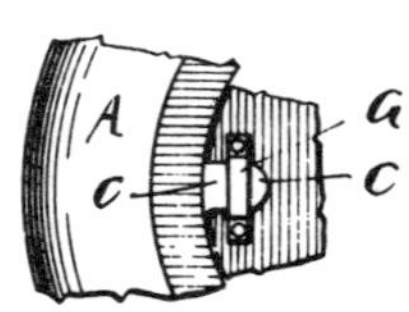

WITNESSES:

Marion Hall

Charles Bles

INVENTOR

A. Sueur

BY

George Raegener

ATTORNEYS.

The music starts when the secret drinker tilts the jug.

(No Model.)

W. L. JUDSON.

CLASP LOCKER OR UNLOCKER FOR SHOES.

No. 504,038. Patented Aug. 29, 1893.

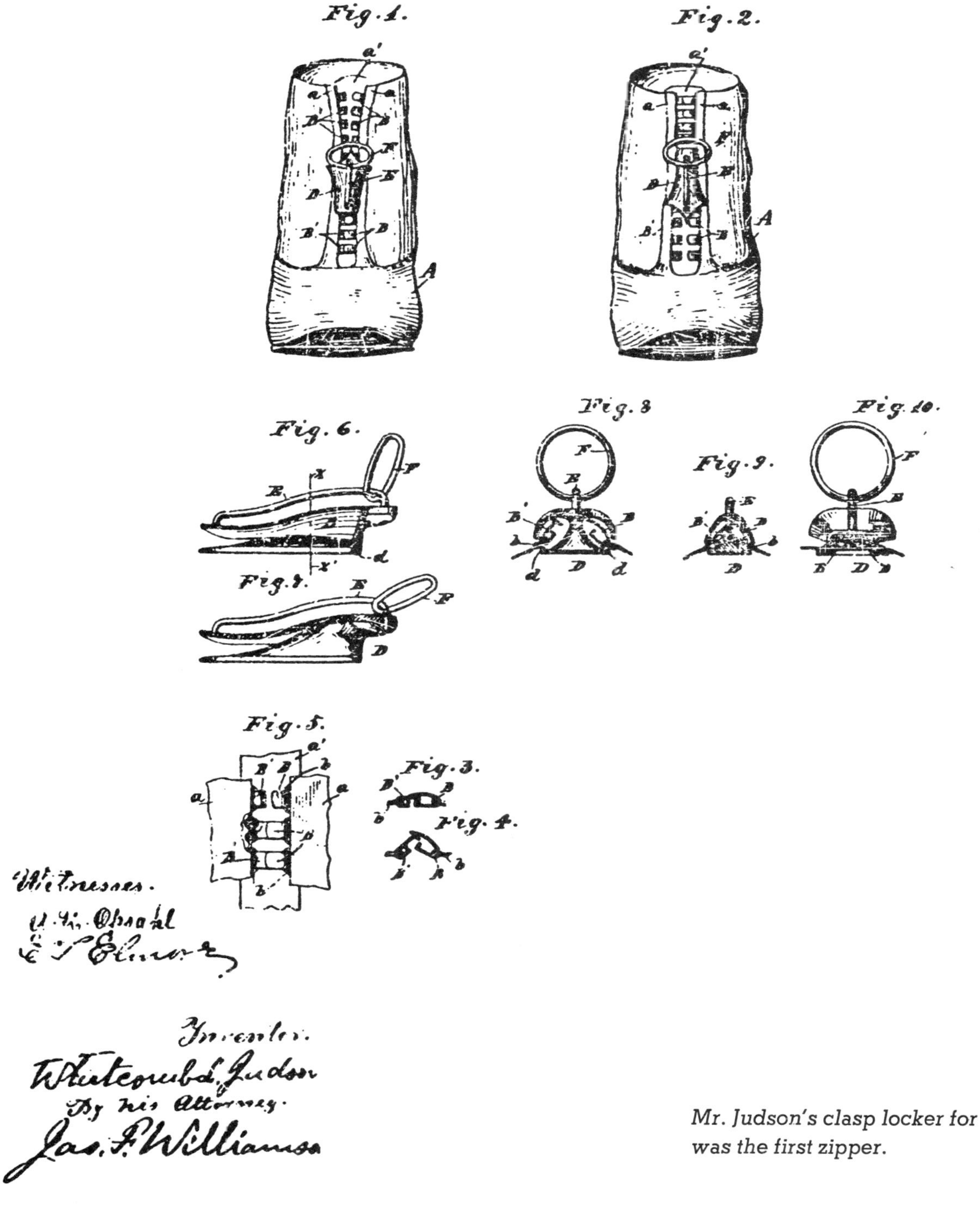

Mr. Judson's clasp locker for shoes was the first zipper.

(No Model.) 2 Sheets—Sheet 1.

H. L. SIMMONS.

RAILROAD TRAIN.

No. 536,360. Patented Mar. 26, 1895.

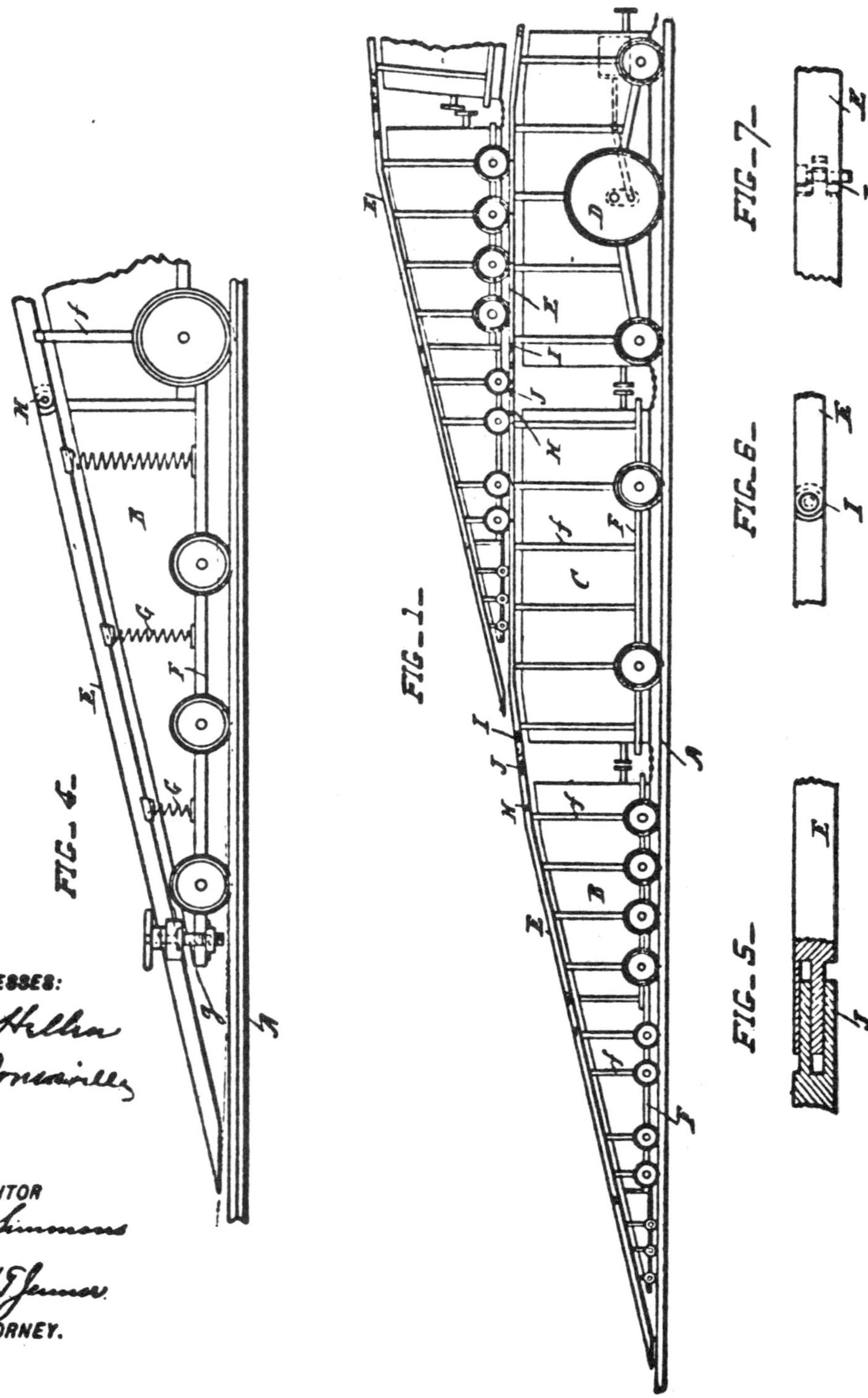

WITNESSES:

W. E. Hellen

H. N. Ronsaville

INVENTOR

Henry L. Simmons

BY

Herbert W. T. Jenner

ATTORNEY.

The first and last cars of this train slant down to the track, so any train it meets or overtakes on the same track will go right over the top.

2 Sheets—Sheet 1.

G. B. SELDEN.

ROAD ENGINE.

No. 549,160. Patented Nov. 5, 1895.

Fig. 1.

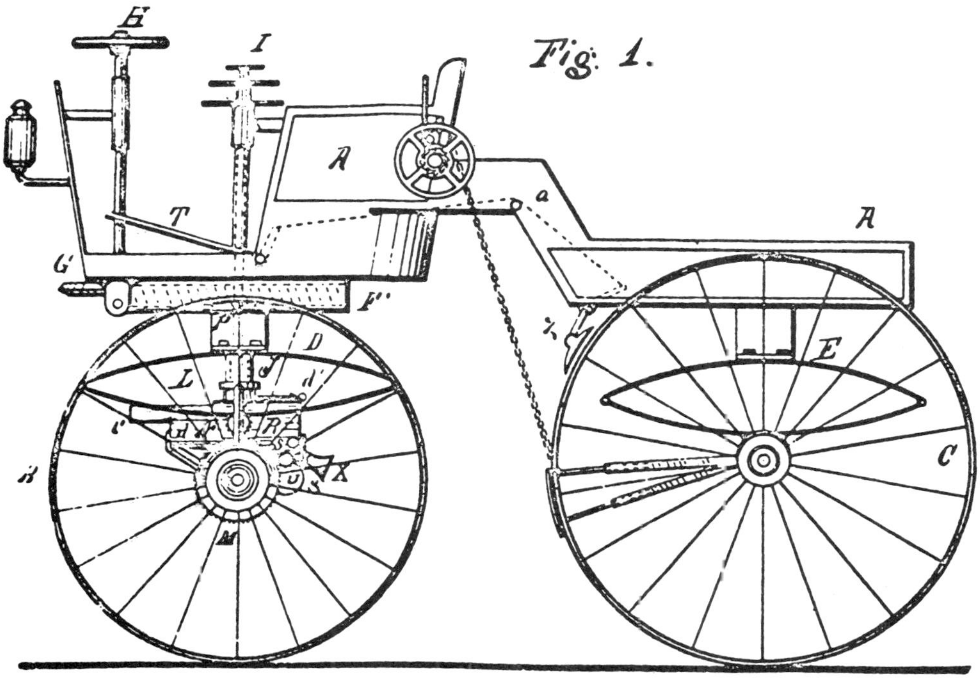

Fig. 2.

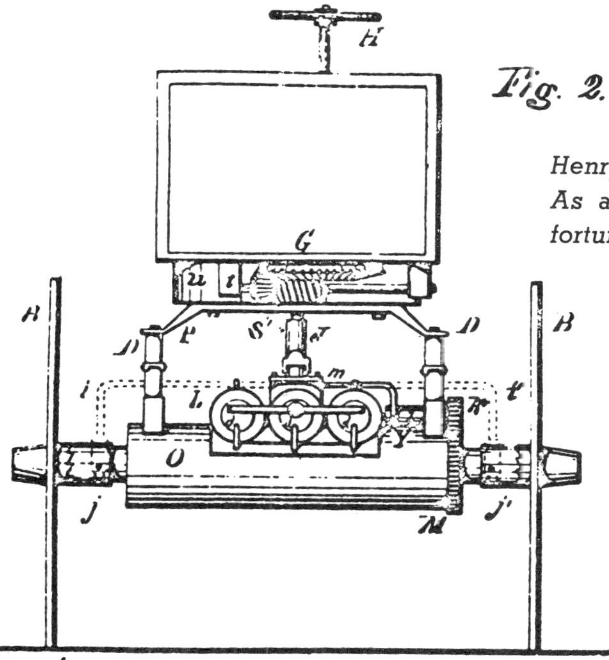

Henry Ford's was not the first car. As a matter of fact, he spent a fortune in court battles.

INVENTOR

Geo. B. Selden

WITNESSES

(No Model.)

R. M. GARDINER.

COMBINED GROCER'S PACKAGE, GRATER, SLICER, AND MOUSE AND FLY TRAP.

No. 586,025. Patented July 6, 1897.

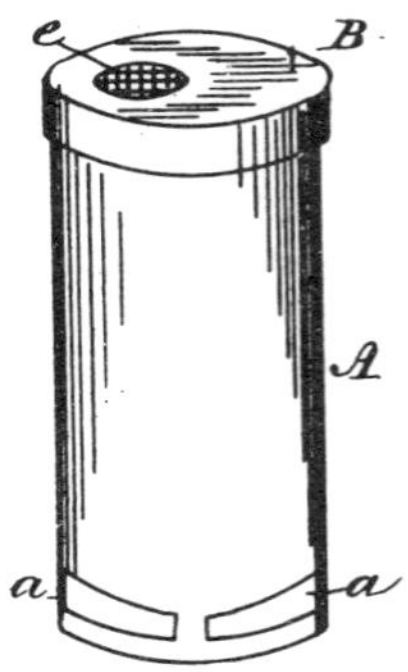

Fig. 1.

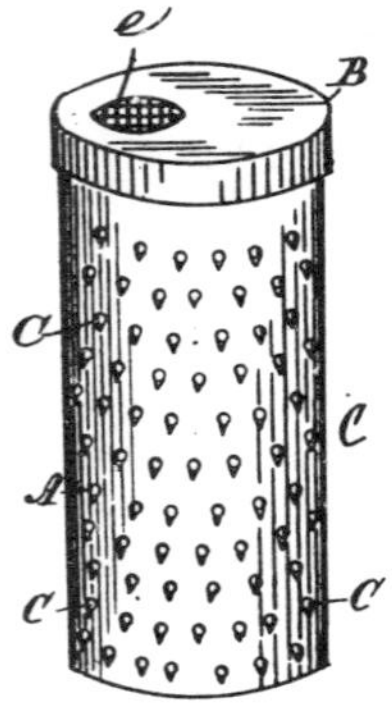

Fig. 2.

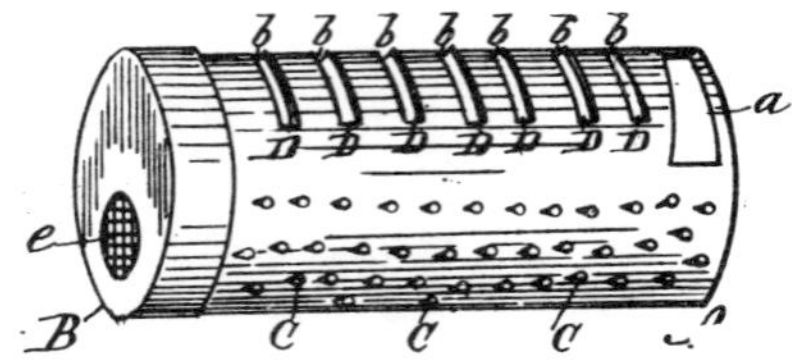

Fig. 3.

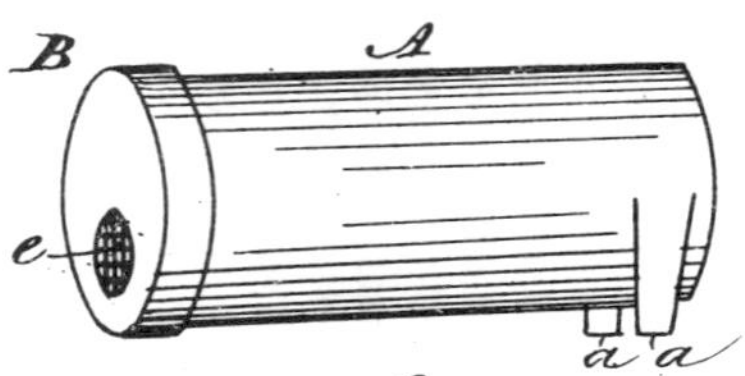

Fig. 4

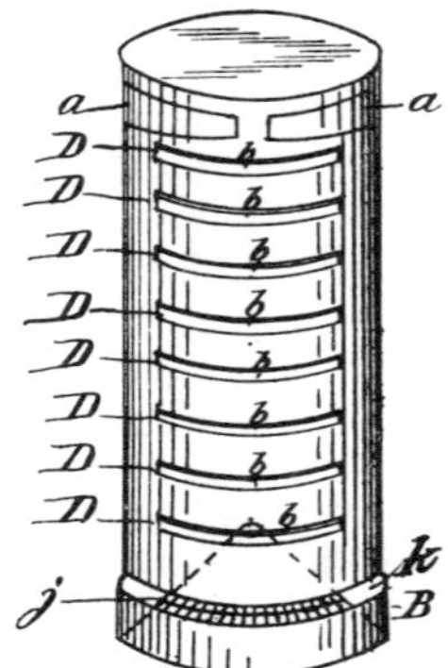

Fig. 7.

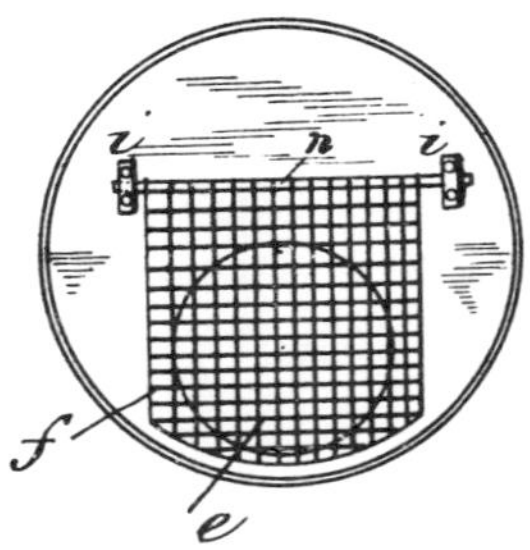

Fig. 8.

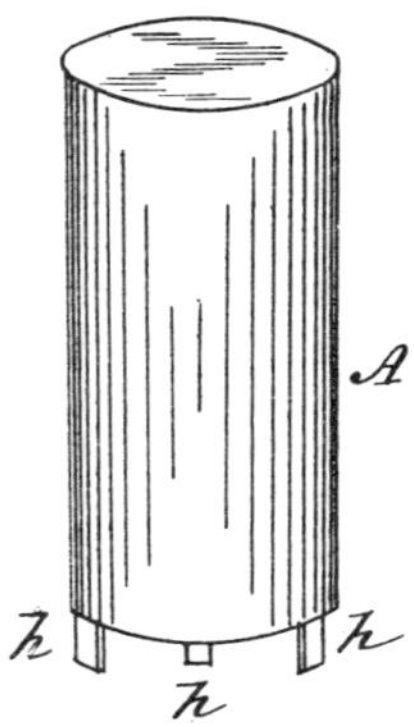

Fig. 5

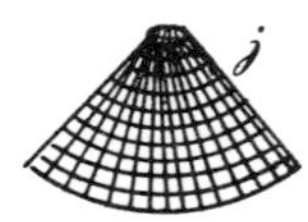

Fig. 6.

Witnesses
D B Pilkey
H. Kane

Inventor
Robert M. Gardiner
By W. Bruce
Atty

This metal cylinder serves a variety of oddly matched purposes. It is a package for groceries, a vegetable slicer and grinder, and a mouse and fly trap.

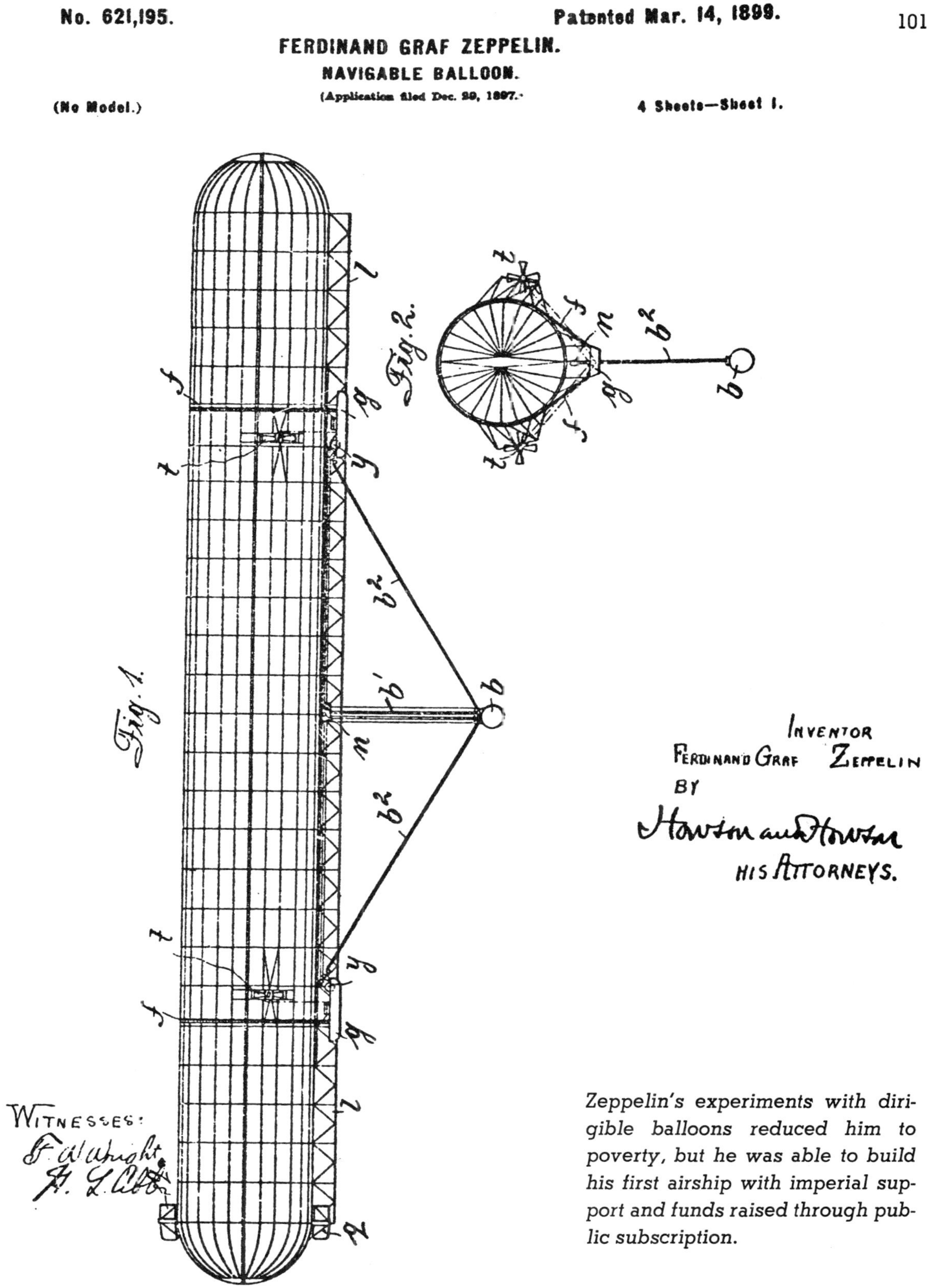

Zeppelin's experiments with dirigible balloons reduced him to poverty, but he was able to build his first airship with imperial support and funds raised through public subscription.

No. 627,693. Patented June 27, 1899.

S. S. HOWARTH.

BICYCLE ATTACHMENT.

(Application filed Jan. 30, 1899.)

(No Model.)

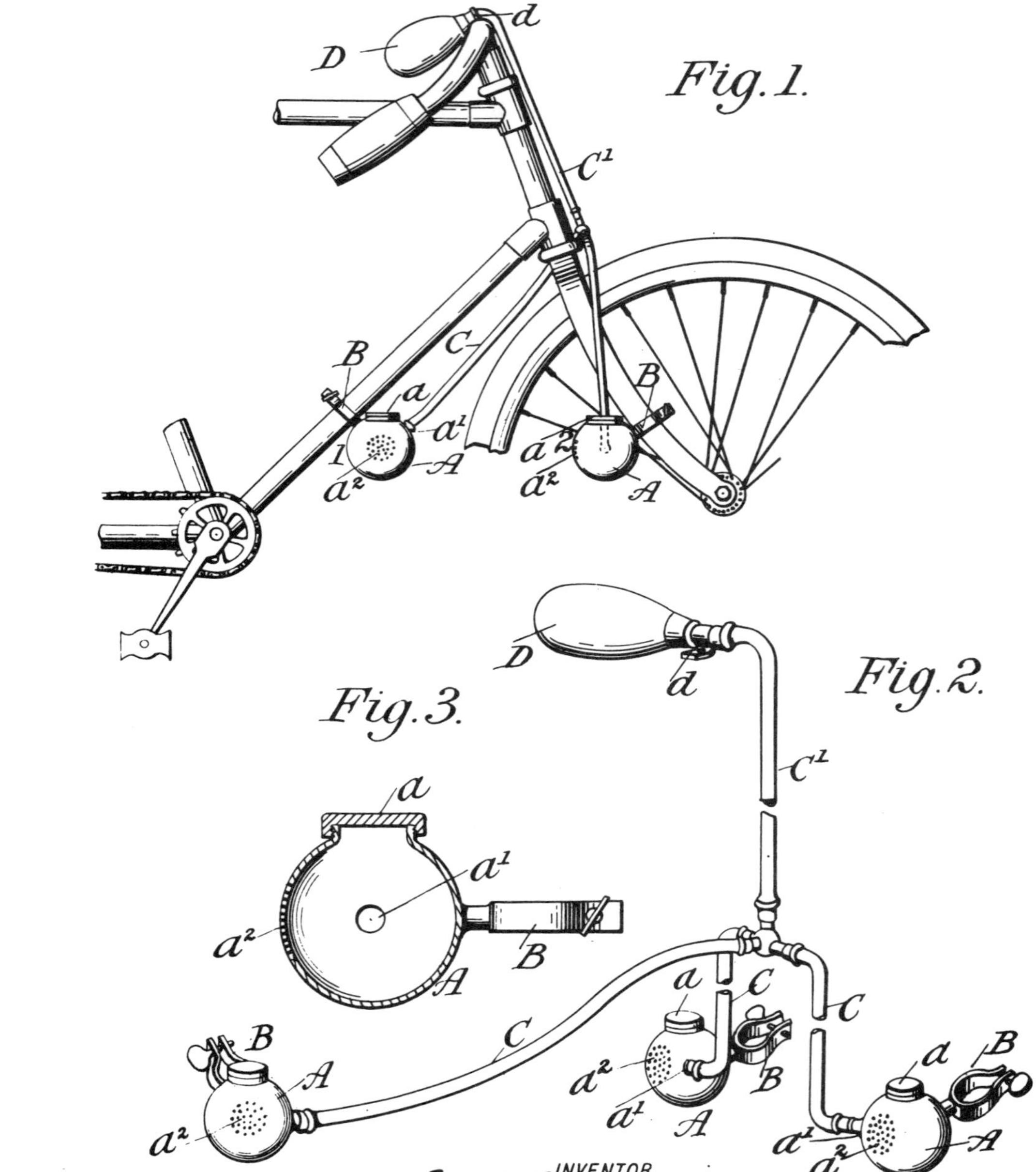

WITNESSES
V. S. Bowen
M. G. MacLean.

INVENTOR
Sarah S. Howarth,
BY
Clark Deemer & Co
ATTORNEYS

When the rider squeezes the bulb, pepper squirts into the dog's face and wards off the attack.

No. 646,065. Patented Mar. 27, 1900.

S. L. BLIGH.

SHAVING DEVICE.

(Application filed Aug. 31, 1899.)

(No Model.)

THIS ELIMINATOR OF FIVE O'CLOCK SHADOW USES SANDPAPER ROLLERS

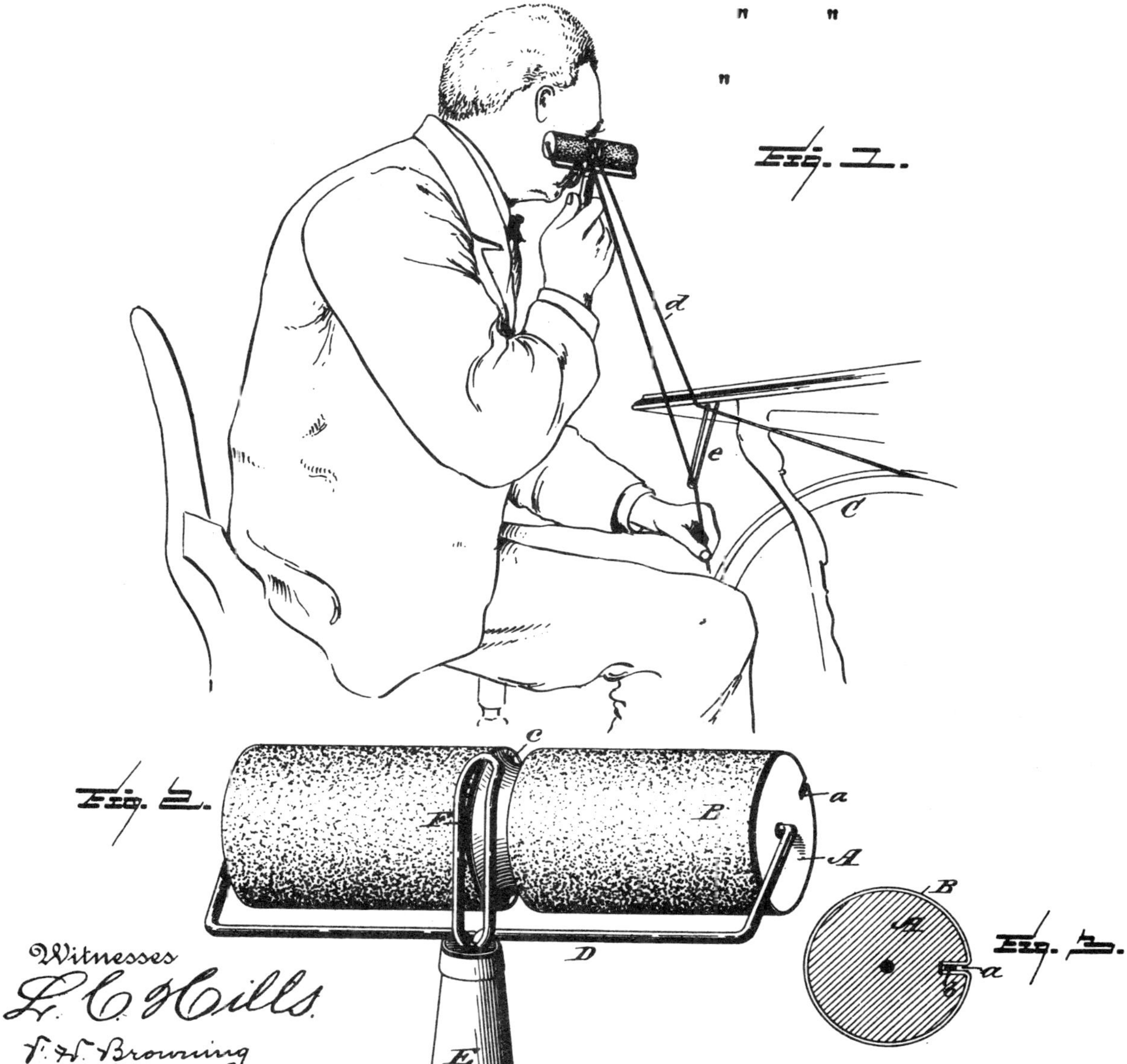

A pedal-powered wheel causes the shaving roller to spin, while the shaver holds it against his face. The roller is covered with emery cloth.

No. 650,082. Patented May 22, 1900.

A. A. NEUBAUER.

BICYCLE ATTACHMENT.

(Application filed Sept. 6, 1899.)

(No Model.) 2 Sheets—Sheet 2.

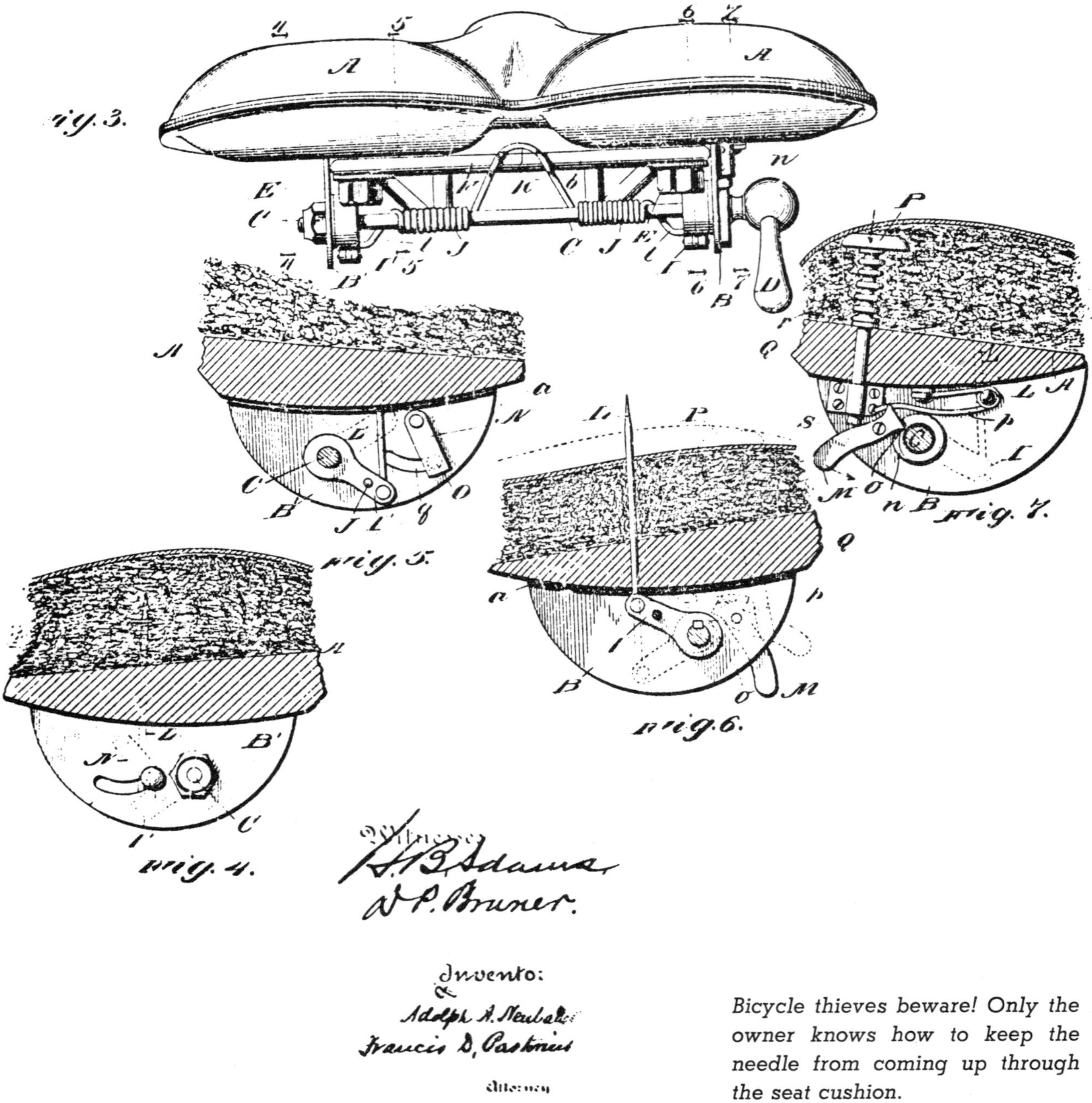

Bicycle thieves beware! Only the owner knows how to keep the needle from coming up through the seat cushion.

No. 643,094. Patented Feb. 6, 1900.

O. A. HENSEL.

ROCKING OR OSCILLATING BATH TUB.

(Application filed Jan. 6, 1899.)

(No Model.) 2 Sheets—Sheet 1.

Fig. 1,

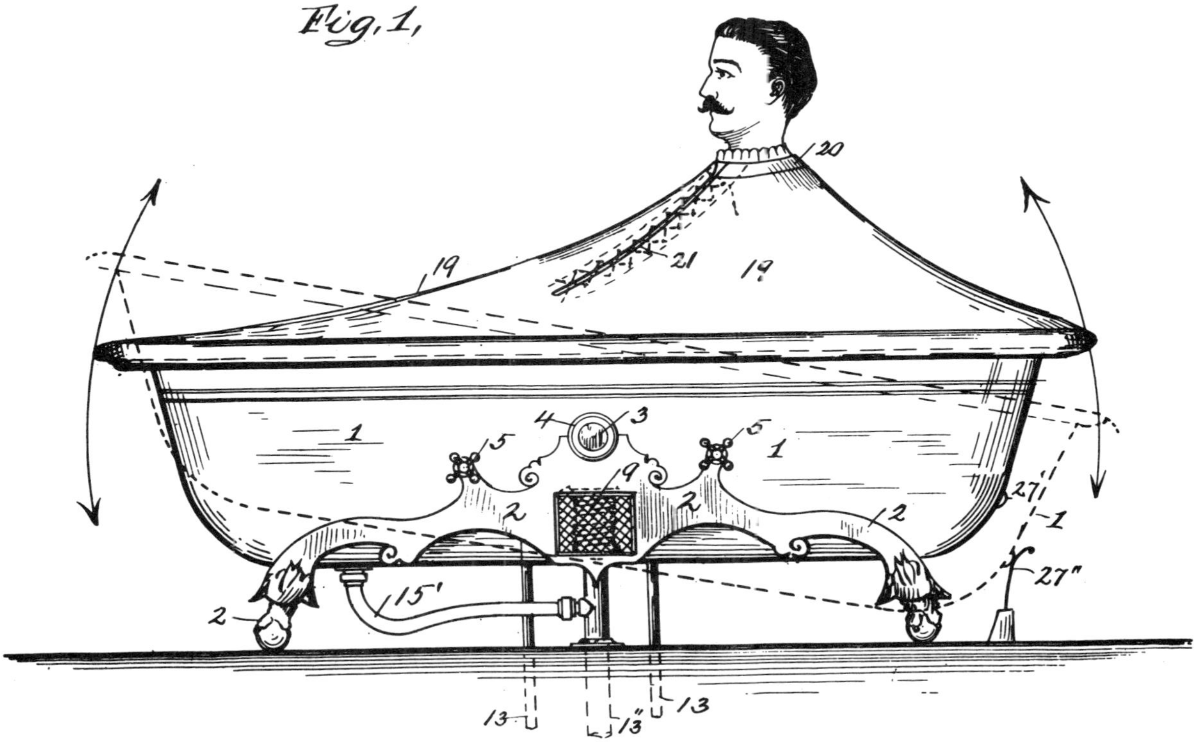

Witnesses:

Wm G. Walter

J. W. Davenport

Inventor.

Otto A. Hensel.

by his attorney

M. E. Harrison.

This rocking bathtub prevents bathtub ring and is supposed to have therapeutic value to the bather.

No. 738,790. PATENTED AUG. 11, 1903.

S. H. MEERZA.

HAT OR THE LIKE.

APPLICATION FILED SEPT. 29, 1902.

NO MODEL.

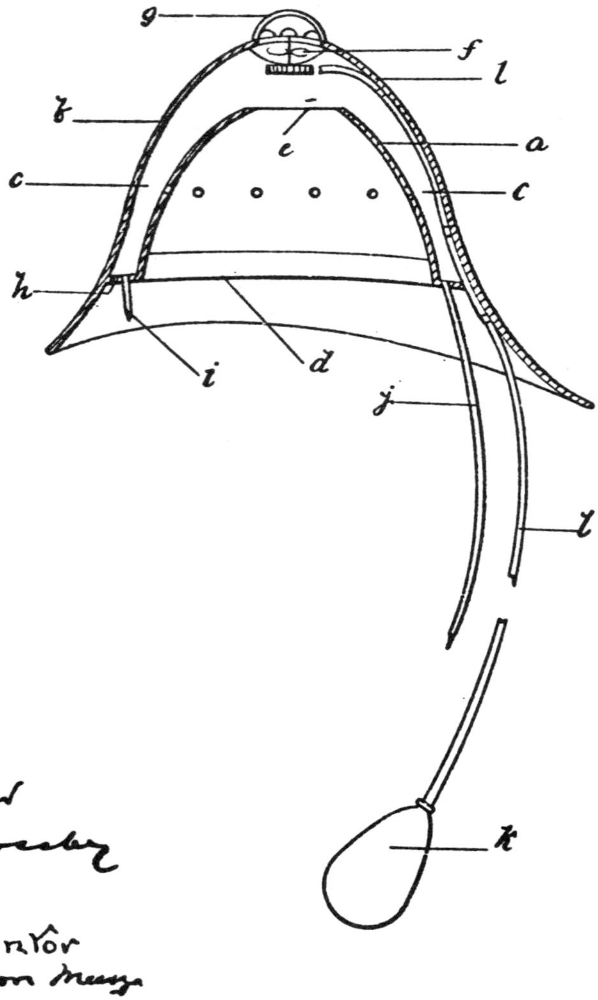

Witnesses
E. H. Sweeter
William Crossley

Inventor
Syed Hozoor Meerza
per Hughes Young
Attorneys

By squeezing the bulb, the wearer can cool his head with a jet of air.

No. 754,353. PATENTED MAR. 8, 1904.

J. E. & J. P. SMITH.

BED PARTITION.

APPLICATION FILED JUNE 16, 1903.

NO MODEL. 2 SHEETS—SHEET 1.

Fig. 1.

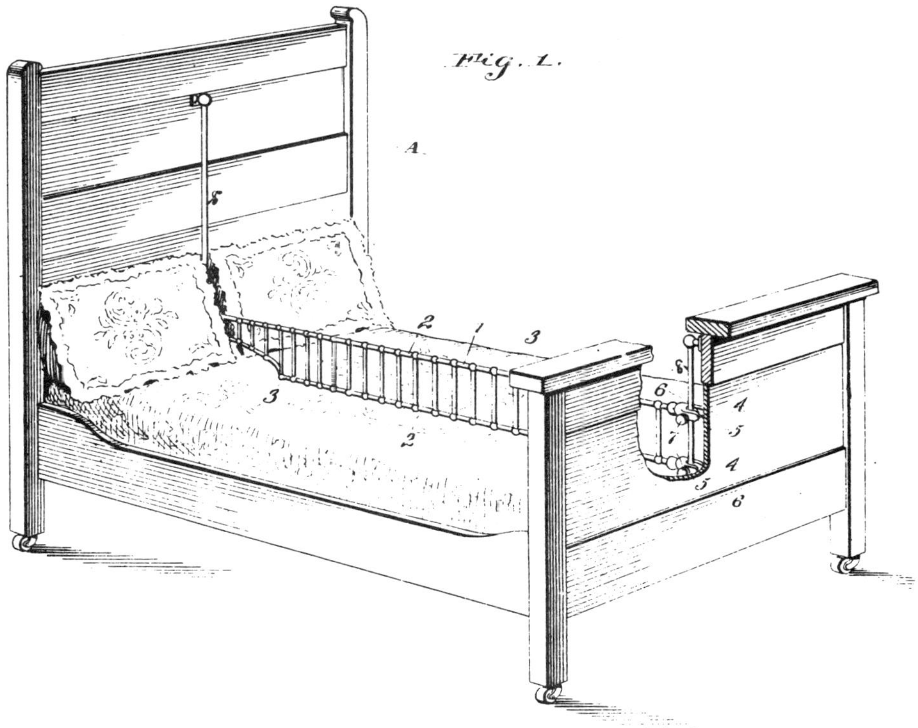

Fig. 2.

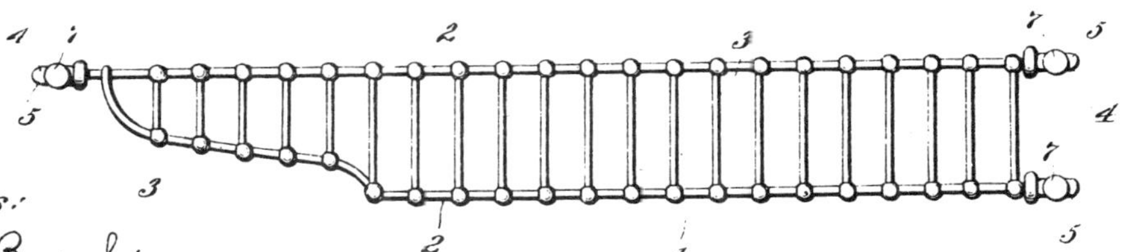

Witnesses:
Isabel Burch.
G. E. McNeil

Fig. 3.

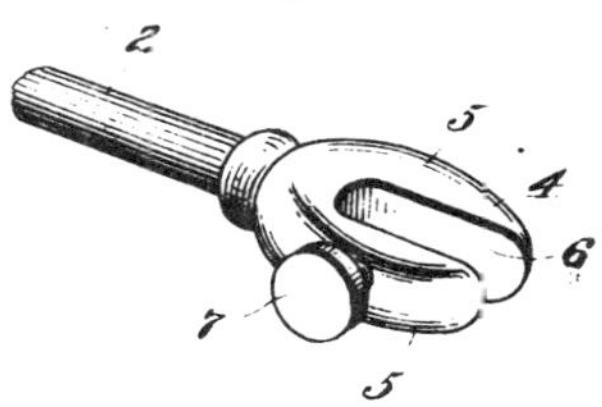

Inventors:
John E. Smith
James P. Smith
By Royal E. Burnham,
Atty.

This clamp-on partition keeps the restless sleeper on his own side of the bed.

No. 807,789. PATENTED DEC. 19, 1905.

Z. T. SWEENEY.

GUIDING DEVICE FOR MOTOR VEHICLES.

APPLICATION FILED JUNE 22, 1905.

POWER STEERING WITH THE HELP OF WIND VANES

Fig. 1.

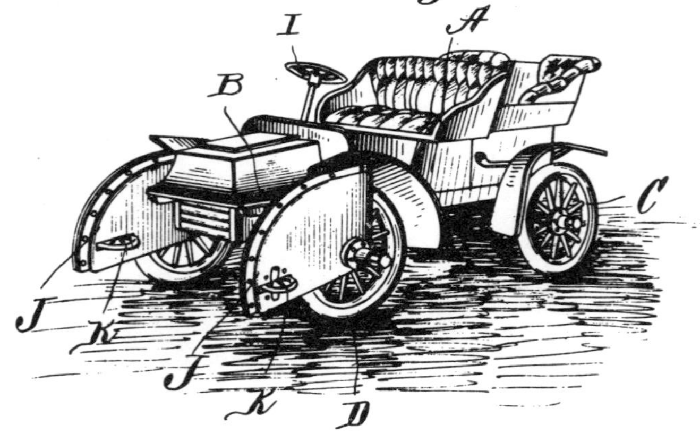

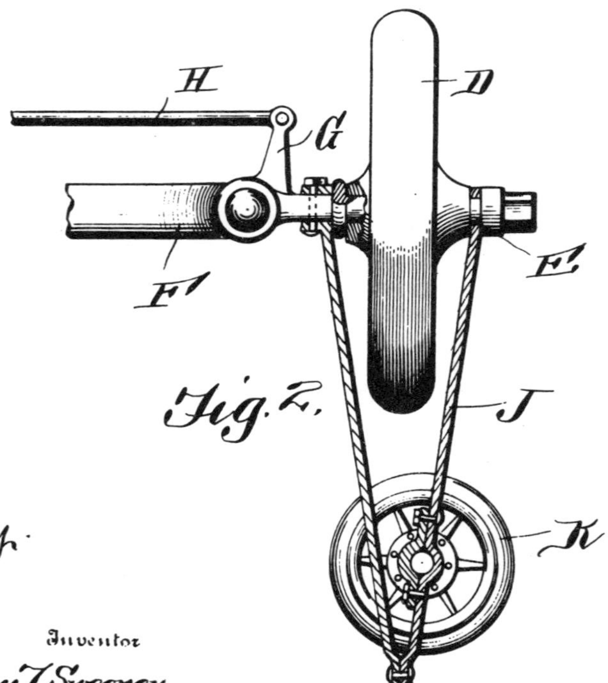

Fig. 2.

Witnesses

Robt. H. Boswell.

Wm J. Whalley.

Inventor

Zachary T. Sweeney.

By Sturtevant & Mason

Attorneys

When the "wind vanes" hit a curb or another object, they cause the wheels to turn away, thus preventing a collision.

No. 821,393. PATENTED MAY 22, 1906.

O. & W. WRIGHT.

FLYING MACHINE.

APPLICATION FILED MAR. 23, 1903.

3 SHEETS—SHEET 1.

FIG. 1.

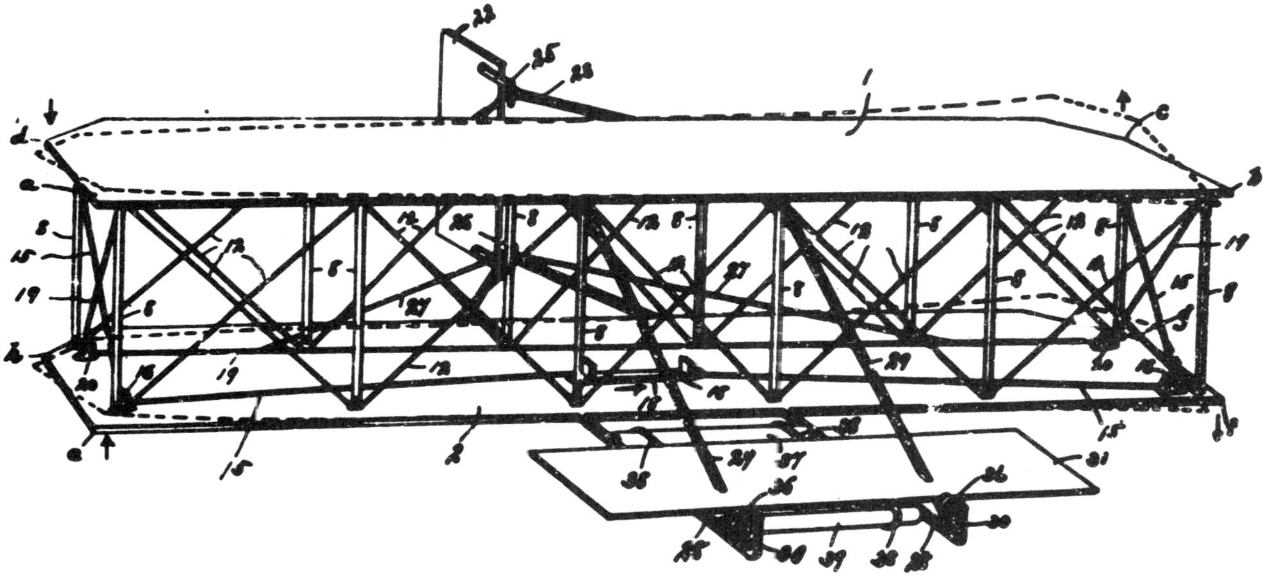

WITNESSES:

William F. Bauer.

INVENTORS.

Orville Wright

Wilbur Wright

BY

ATTORNEY.

The Wright Brothers' Kitty Hawk flight, December 17, 1903, was shorter than the distance from cockpit to tail in a modern DC-10.

No. 775,134. PATENTED NOV. 15, 1904.

K. C. GILLETTE.

RAZOR.

APPLICATION FILED DEC. 3, 1901.

NO MODEL.

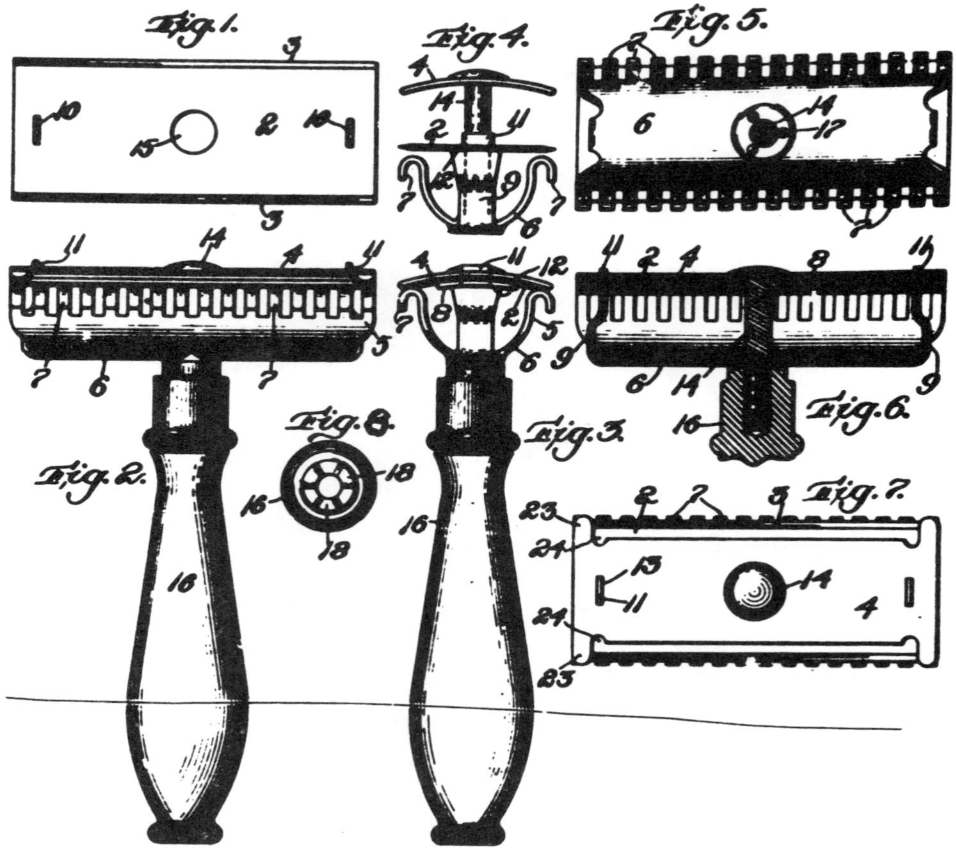

Witnesses:

Ruby M. Banfield

Inventor:

King C. Gillette,

By

E. D. Chadwick,

Attorney.

Gillette's razor allowed users to buy one holder and replace the blades whenever they became dull.

No. 883,611. PATENTED MAR. 31, 1908.

J. BARAD & E. E. MARKOFF.

DEVICE EMPLOYED FOR EXTERMINATING RATS, MICE, AND OTHER ANIMALS.

APPLICATION FILED DEC. 16, 1907.

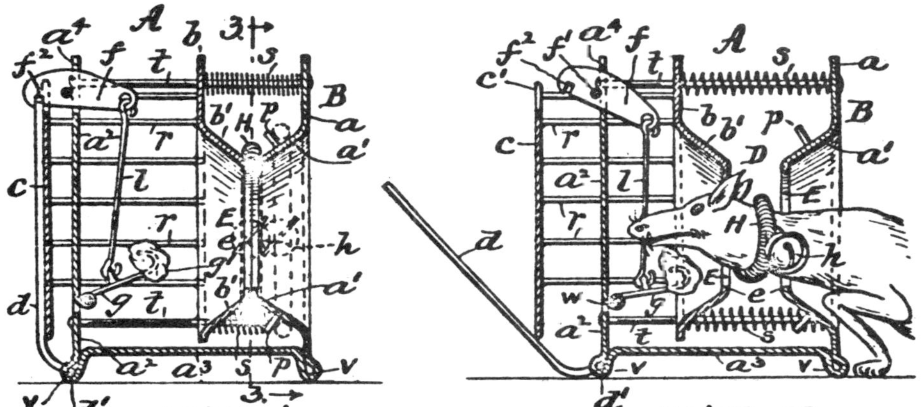

FIG. 1. FIG. 2.

A DEVICE FOR PUTTING A BELL ON A MOUSE SO IT CAN BE FOUND BY A NEARSIGHTED CAT

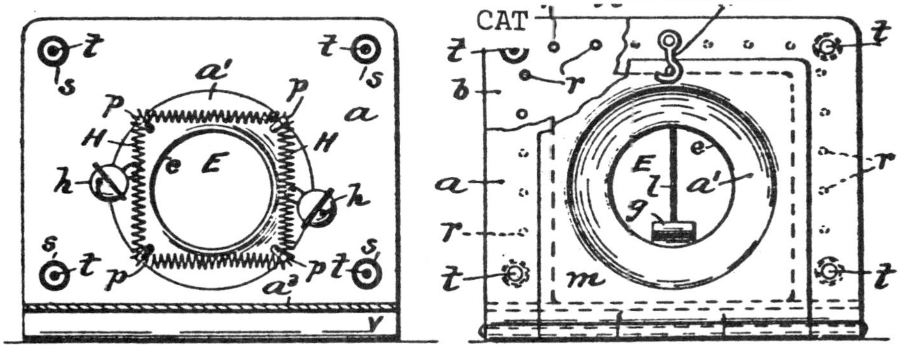

FIG. 3. FIG. 4.

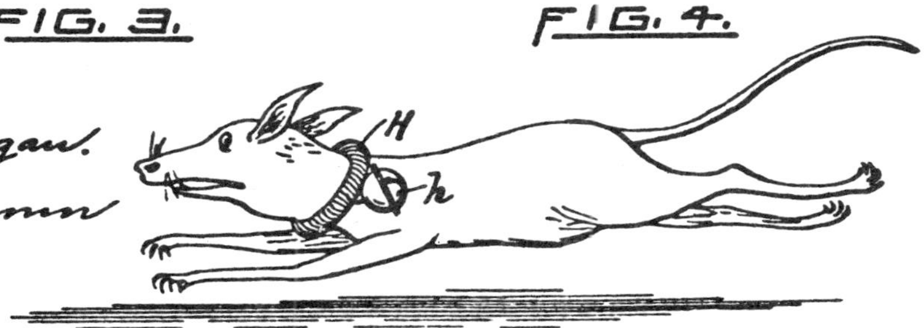

WITNESSES:

C. T. Hennigan.

Calvin H. Brown

INVENTORS.

FIG. 5. Joseph Barad

Edward E. Markoff.

By Geo. H. Remington.

Attorney.

This device puts a bell on a mouse, so it is easier for the cat to make the catch.

S. A. MERKLEY.
EGG MARKING DEVICE.
APPLICATION FILED APR. 18, 1910.

970,074. Patented Sept. 13, 1910.

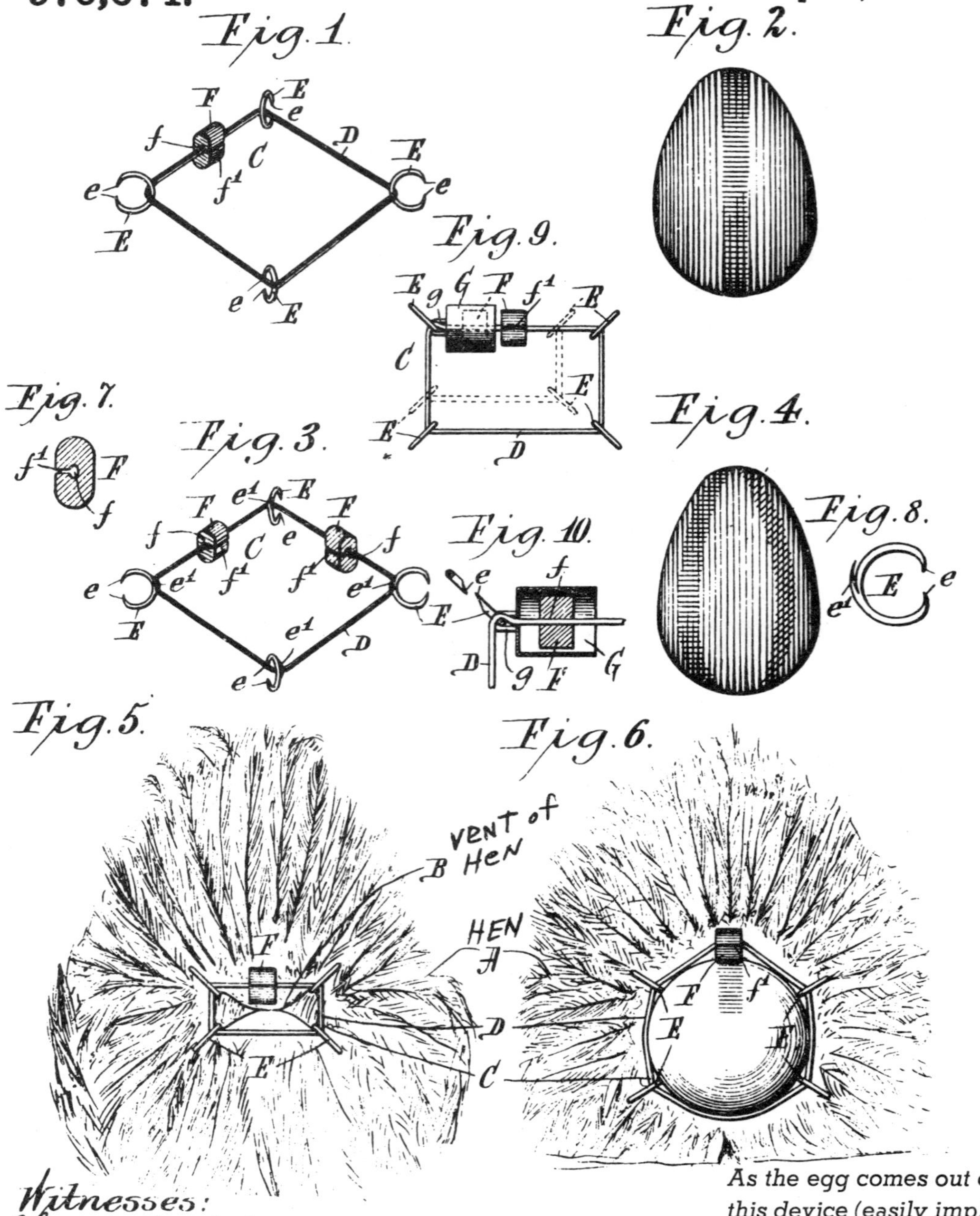

Witnesses:
Christ Feinle, Jr.,
Jacob L. Oberst, Jr.

Stanley A. Merkley, Inventor.

As the egg comes out of the chute, this device (easily implanted in the hen) imprints it with a special mark so the farmer will know which hens are laying and which are not.

A. ZUKOR.
BURGLAR ALARM.
APPLICATION FILED JULY 22, 1912.

1,046,533. Patented Dec. 10, 1912.

2 SHEETS—SHEET 1.

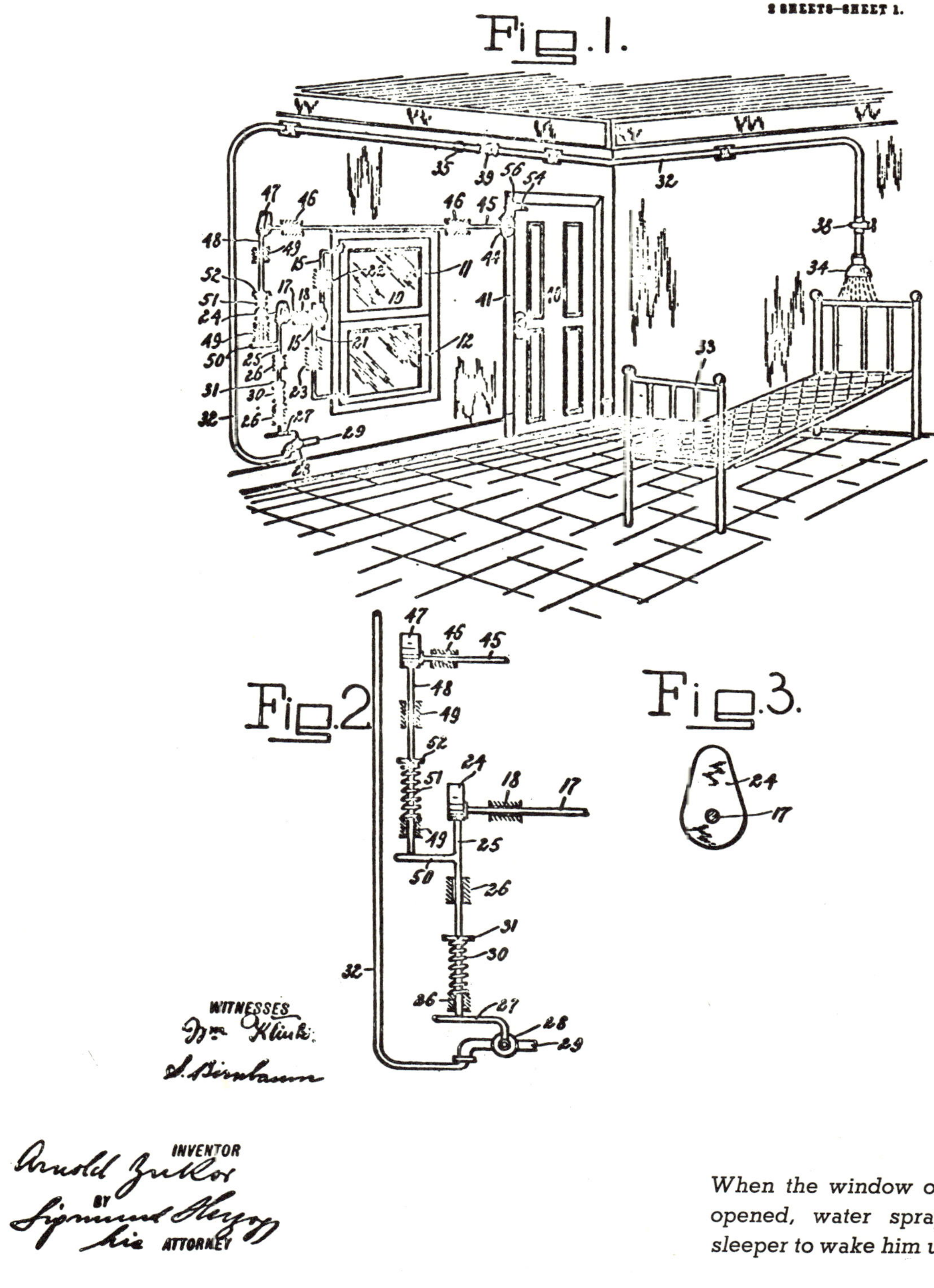

When the window or the door is opened, water sprays onto the sleeper to wake him up.

E. M. WARING.
SUCTION CLEANING APPARATUS.
APPLICATION FILED MAR. 16, 1909.

1,105,942. Patented Aug. 4, 1914.

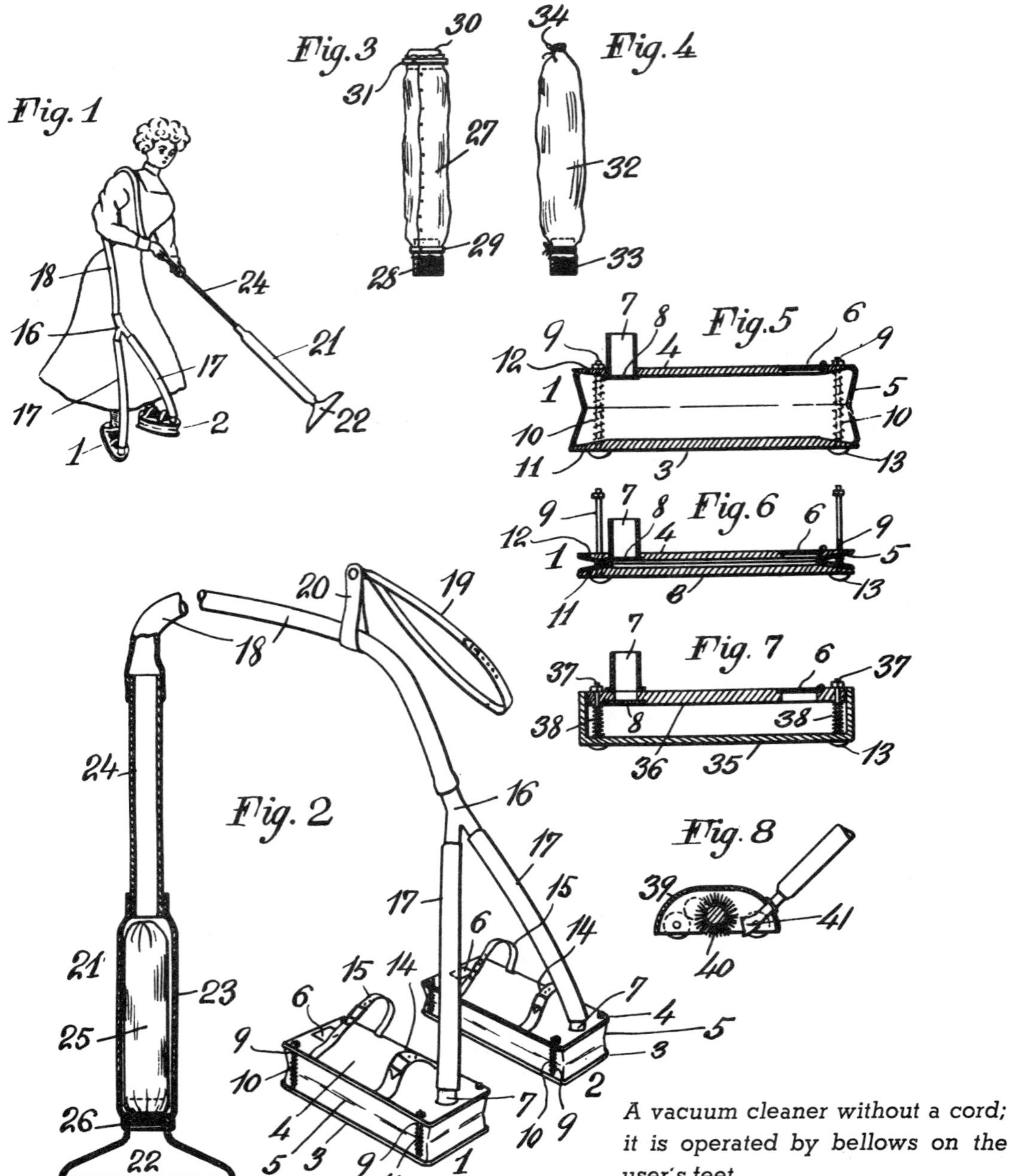

A vacuum cleaner without a cord; it is operated by bellows on the user's feet.

Witnesses
M. M. Riemann.
H. G. Leard.

Edward M. Waring Inventor
By his Attorney
Ivan E. A. Konigsberg.

W. P. ZEIGLER.
ARTIFICIAL FISH BAIT.
APPLICATION FILED APR. 23, 1915.

1,180,753. **Patented Apr. 25, 1916.**

FIG. 1.

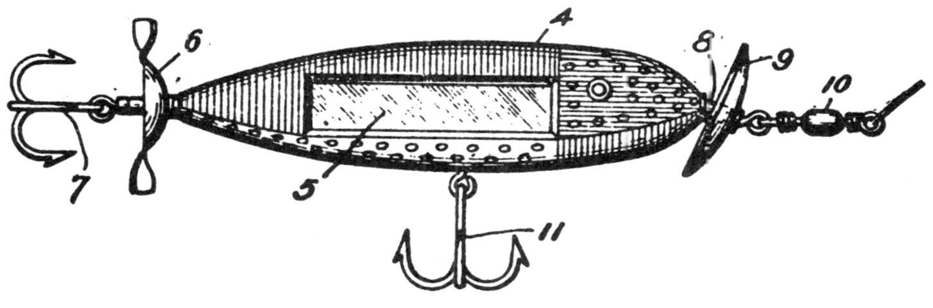

FIG. 2.

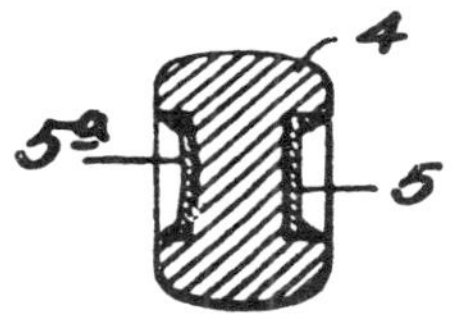

Flashing metal attracts a fish, who sees his own image in the mirror. Thinking it's another fish after his prey, his fighting spirit comes to the fore and he jumps at the bait.

The attractiveness of the bait for the fish is increased by making the disks 6 and 9 of highly polished metal. The glitter and flashing lights occasioned by these and by the mirror are well known attractives; but the mirror 5 is an additional feature that insures the effectiveness of the bait in the following manner: A male fish seeing his image upon looking therein will appear to see another fish approach it from the opposite side with the intent to seize the bait, and this will not only arouse his warlike spirit, but also appeal to his greed, and he will seize the bait quickly in order to defeat the approaching rival. In case the fish is suspected of cowardice I may make the mirror of convex form, as shown at 5a, in order that the rival or antagonist may appear to be smaller. In the case of a female fish the attractiveness of a mirror is too well known to need discussion. Thus the bait appeals to the ruling passion of both sexes, and renders it very certain and efficient in operation . . .

WITNESS

J. Herbert Bradley.

INVENTOR

William P. Zeigler

By F. W. H. Clay, atty.

APPLICATION FILED MAR. 15, 1916.

1,187,218. Patented June 13, 1916.

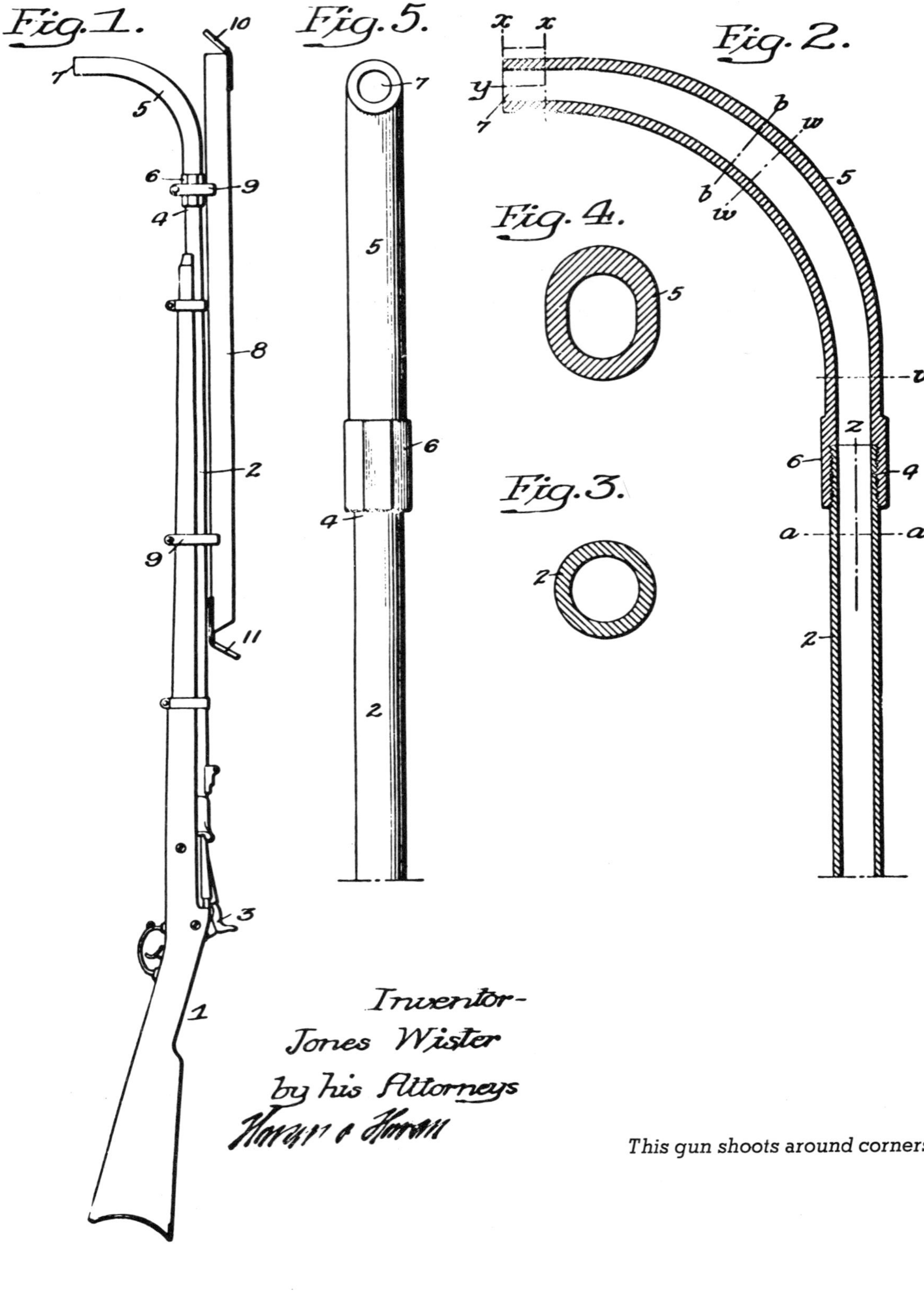

This gun shoots around corners.

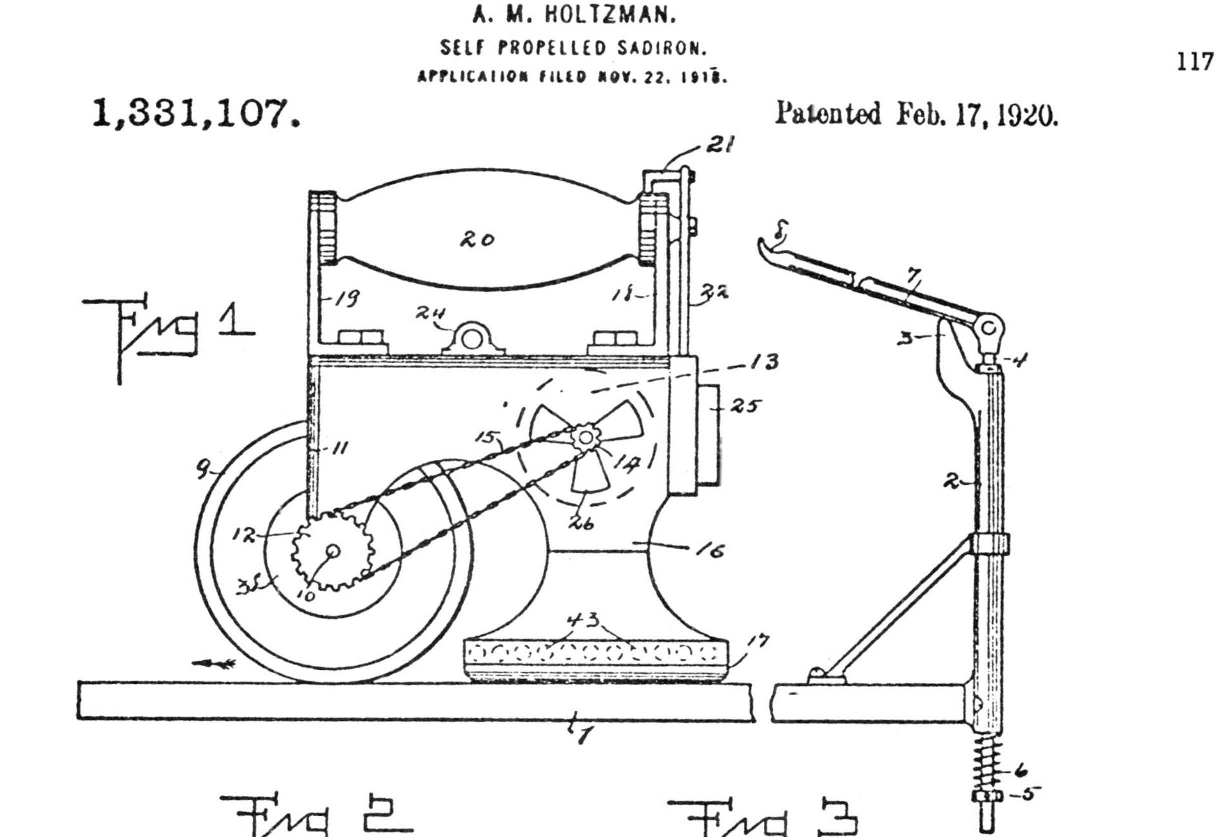

A SELF-PROPELLED IRON FOR WEAK OR TIRED HOUSEWIVES

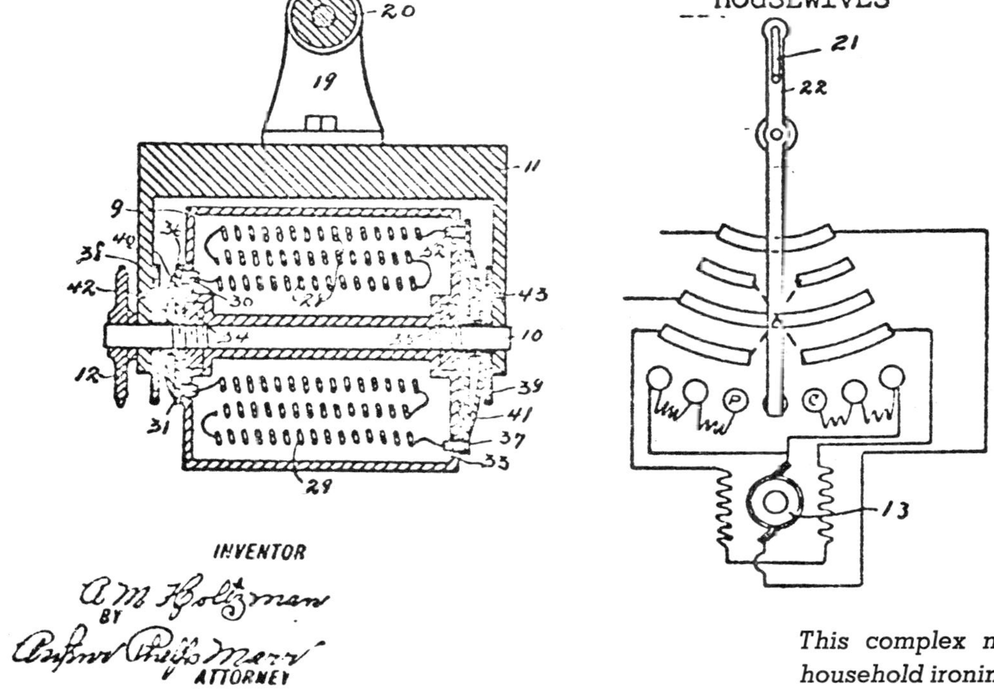

This complex machine does the household ironing.

H. HOUDINI.

DIVER'S SUIT.

APPLICATION FILED JUNE 30, 1917.

1,370,316. Patented Mar. 1, 1921.

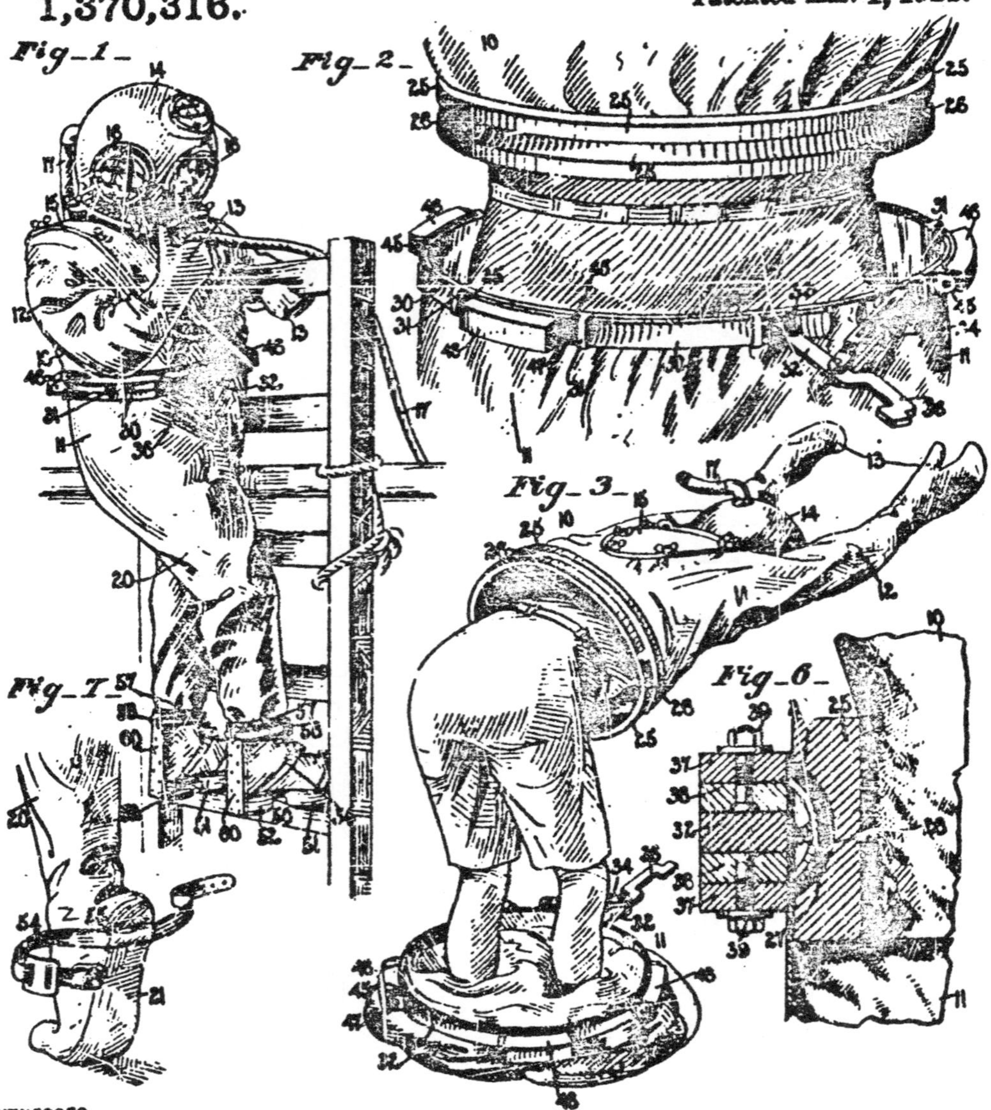

WITNESSES

Frank C. Palmer

Geo. G. Hoertz

INVENTOR

H. Houdini

BY Munn & Co

ATTORNEYS

A diver can put on Harry Houdini's diver's suit without assistance, and he can easily get out of it underwater for a quick swim to the surface. The suit allows divers to go deeper and faster than they could with other suits.

E. SWENSEN.
ELECTRICAL SYSTEM FOR USE IN CATTLE STALLS.
APPLICATION FILED MAY 20, 1920.

1,411,312. **Patented Apr. 4, 1922.**

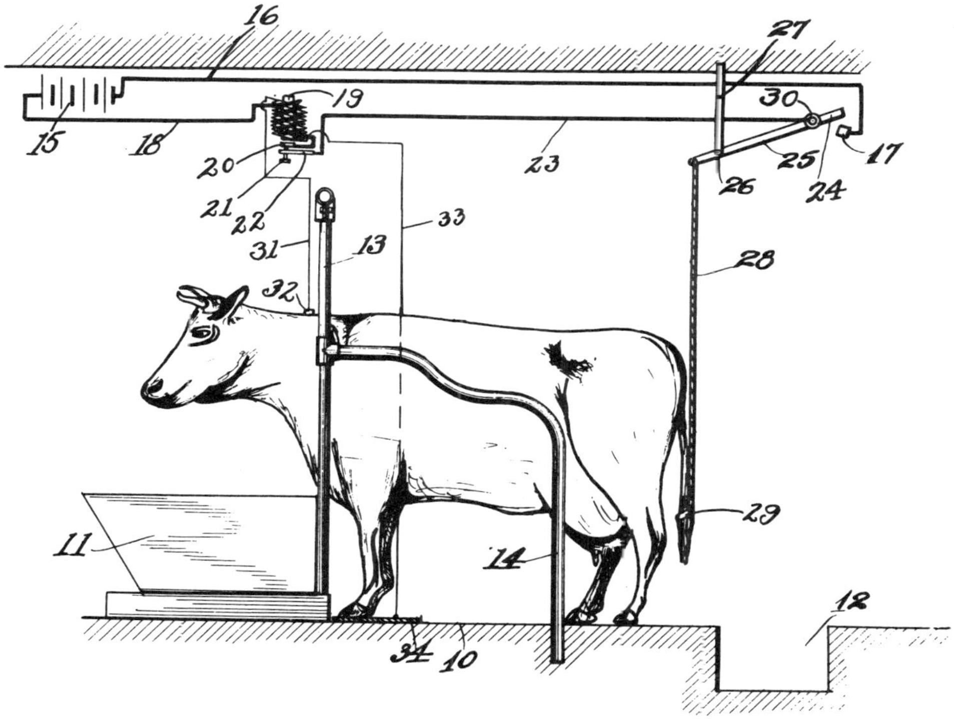

WITNESS:
Wm Casati

INVENTOR.
Elmer Swensen
BY
Jones, Addington, Ames & Seibold
ATTORNEYS.

When the cow lifts her tail to go to the bathroom, she is shocked, causing her to back up and use the ditch.

May 3, 1938. T. L. HOLLISTER **2,116,434**

DEVICE FOR STORING EXHAUST GASES IN AUTOMOBILES

Filed July 29, 1937 2 Sheets-Sheet 1

Fig. 1.

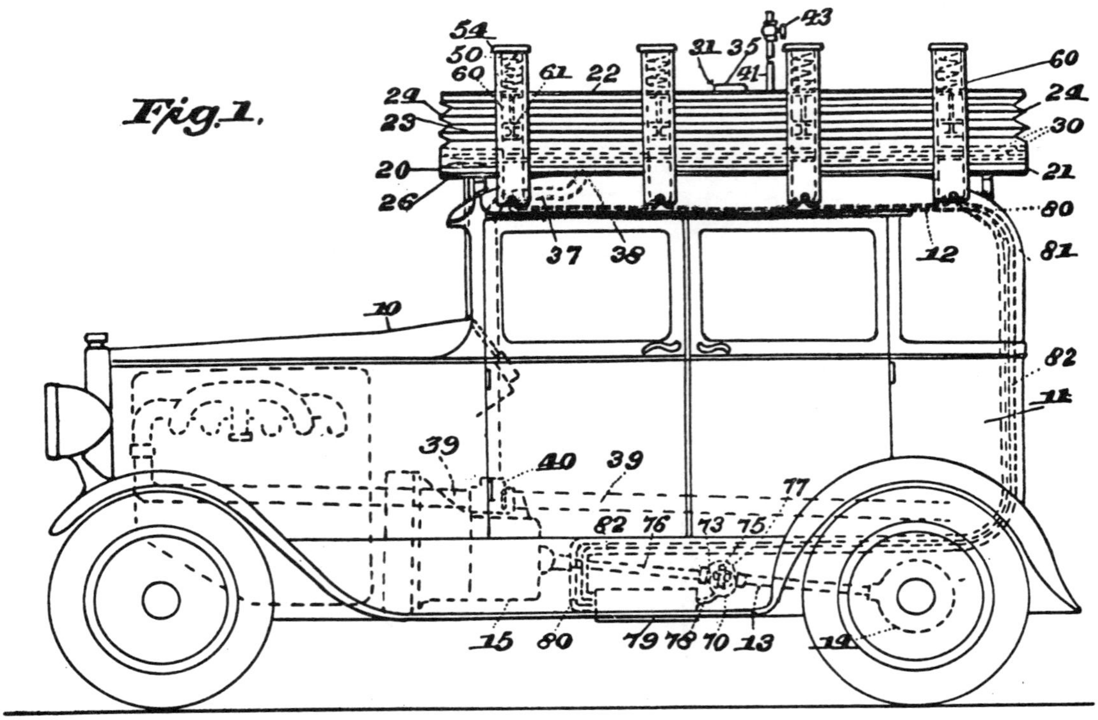

Fig. 2.

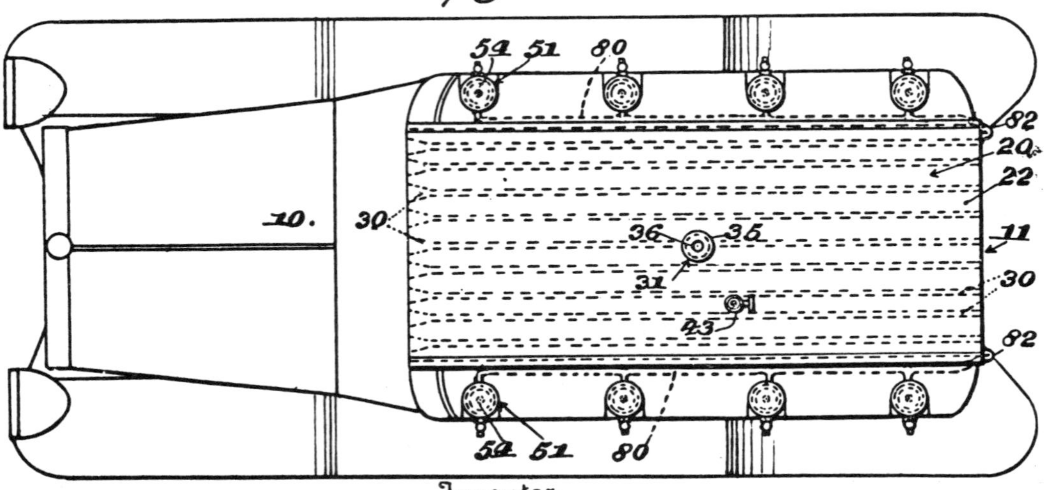

Inventor

Thomas Lloyd Hollister

By Munn, Anderson & Liddy Attorneys

This early anti-pollution device catches exhaust in an inflatable bag on top of the car. When the bag is full, the driver stops and empties it at a roadside collection station.

April 16, 1946. C. E. SHORT ET AL **2,398,471**

POWER UNITS FOR AMUSEMENT DEVICES AND THE LIKE

Filed May 15, 1945 2 Sheets—Sheet 1

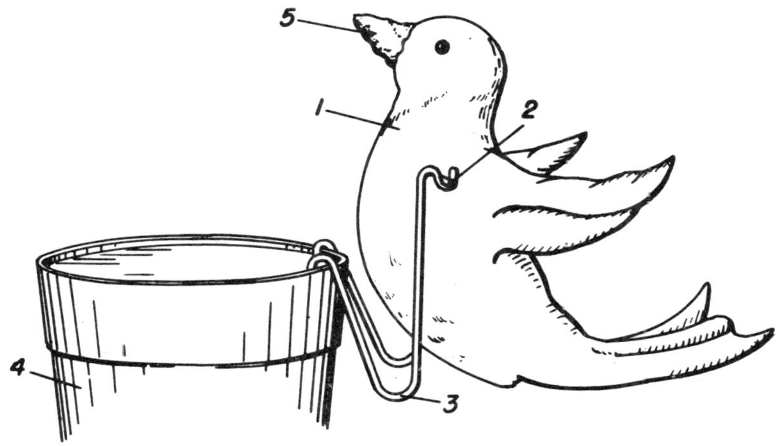

FIGURE 1

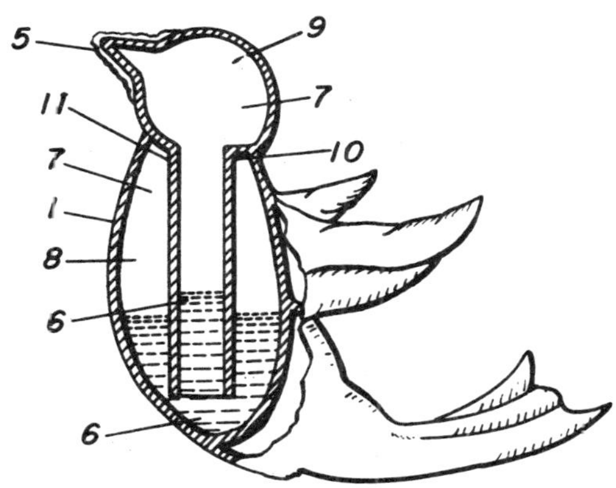

FIGURE 2

Edward M. Brown, Jr.
Charles E. Short
INVENTORS

BY Ernest M. Symmes
ATTORNEY

Here's how the dunking bird works: Moisture on the beak causes the gas inside of the bird to condense to a liquid, and the unbalance causes the bird to sit upright, with its beak out of water. Room temperature converts the liquid back to gas, and the bird falls over again to get another drink.

Oct. 7, 1958 J. A. ROSS 2,854,942

GARAGE INDICATOR TO AVOID AUTOMOBILE OVERSHOOTING

Filed Aug. 27, 1958

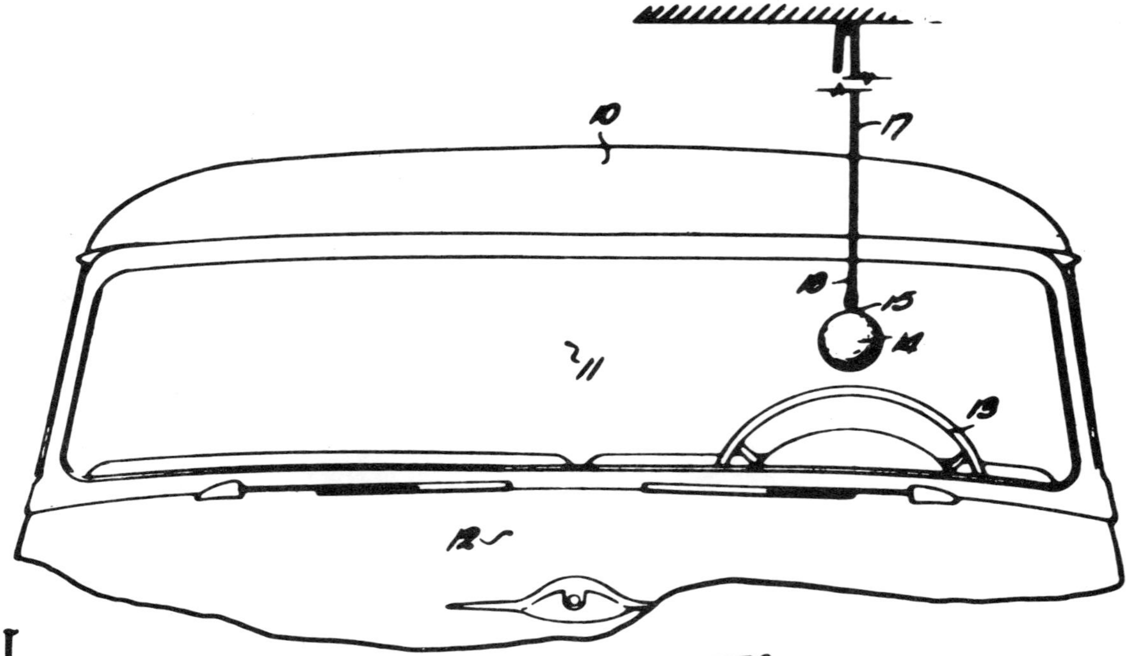

Fig. 1.

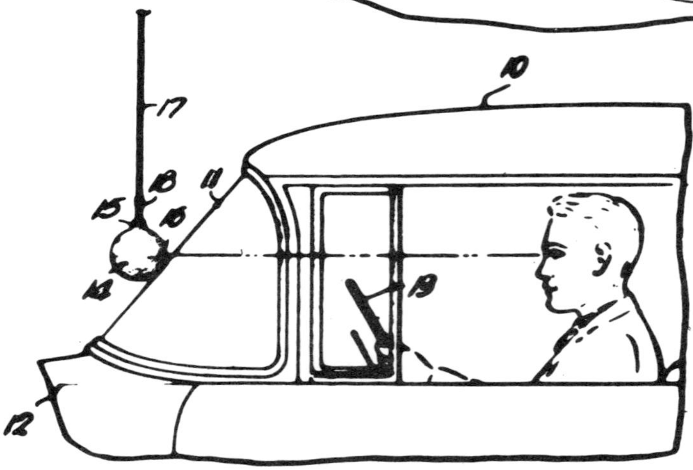

Fig. 2.

INVENTOR
John A. Ross

BY
Thos. E. Scofield
ATTORNEY.

This easy-to-install device helps you park your car in the right spot every time.

United States Patent [19]

James

[11] **3,802,945**

[45] **Apr. 9, 1974**

[54] **HEAT SENSITIVE NOVELTY DEVICE**

[76] Inventor: **Bill G. James,** 1895 Cordilleros Rd., Redwood City, Calif. 94062

[22] Filed: **Oct. 14, 1971**

[21] Appl. No.: **189,188**

[52] **U.S. Cl.**.................. **161/5,** 23/230 LC, 40/28 R, 161/6, 161/139, 161/DIG. 5, 161/410, 252/408, 350/160 R

[51] **Int. Cl.**............................ **B44f 9/08,** B01j 13/02

[58] **Field of Search**............. 252/408; 161/1, 3.5, 5, 161/6, 139, DIG. 1, DIG. 5, 408–410; 350/160 LC; 23/230 LC; 40/28 C, 28 R

[56] **References Cited**

UNITED STATES PATENTS

3,585,381	6/1971	Hodson et al.	161/410 X
3,574,043	4/1971	Luber et al.	161/5
3,637,291	1/1972	Kessler et al.	40/28 C
3,647,280	3/1972	Klein et al.	350/160 R
3,720,623	3/1973	Cartmell et al.	23/230 LC

Primary Examiner—Harold Ansher
Attorney, Agent, or Firm—John J. Leavitt

[57] **ABSTRACT**

A novelty device which utilizes the iridescing qualities of liquid crystalline material to effect variations in colorations of the device upon application of different temperatures.

7 Claims, 9 Drawing Figures

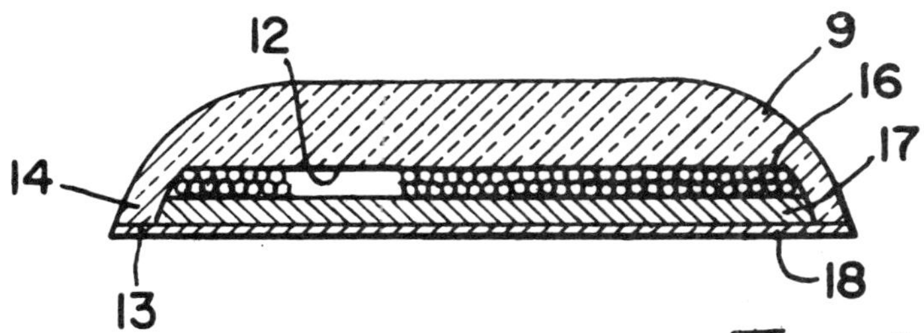

Supposedly, the ring, earring, tie clip, or whatever turns green, gray, black, or blue depending on the mood of the wearer.

FIG. 1.

United States Patent [19]

Slemp

[11] **3,823,494**

[45] **July 16, 1974**

[54] **FOOTWEAR WITH HEEL AND TOE POSITIONS REVERSED**

[76] Inventor: **Cecil Slemp,** Rt. 1, Box 120-A, Jarrettsville, Md. 21084

[22] Filed: **Nov. 20, 1973**

[21] Appl. No.: **417,604**

[52] **U.S. Cl.** .... **36/2.5 R**
[51] **Int. Cl.** **A43b**
[58] **Field of Search** .... 36/1, 2.5 R, 2.5 E, 25 R

[56] **References Cited**

UNITED STATES PATENTS

3,170,248 2/1965 Levine .... 36/2.5 R
3,402,485 9/1968 McMorrow 36/1
3,463,163 8/1969 Matles .... 36/2.5 R

Primary Examiner—Patrick D. Lawson
Attorney, Agent, or Firm—John F. McClellan, Sr.

[57] **ABSTRACT**

Footwear having heel and toe positions reversed so that the wearer leaves tracks indicating a travel direction opposite to the actual direction of travel.

9 Claims, 9 Drawing Figures

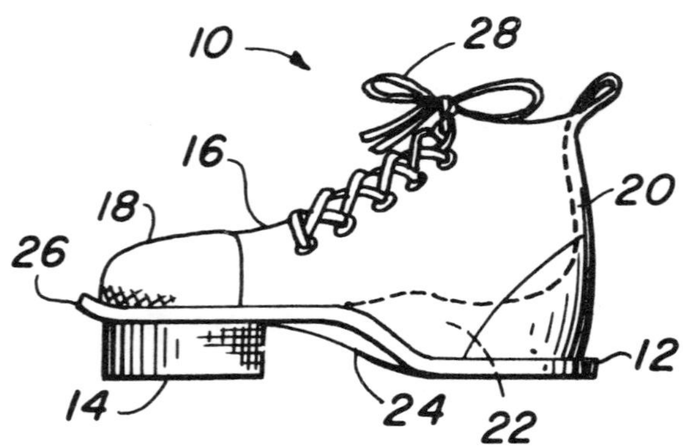

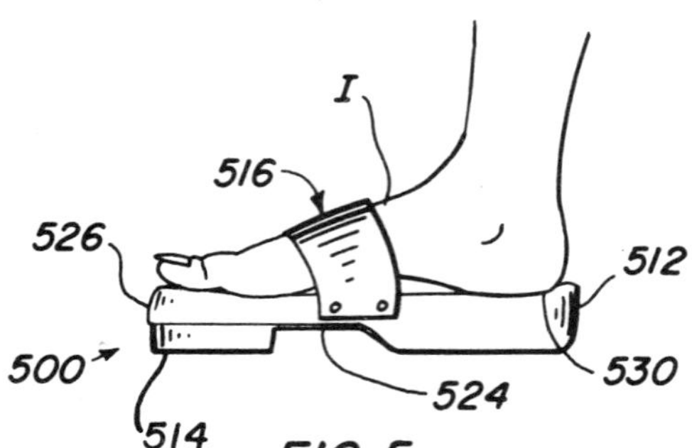

FIG. 5

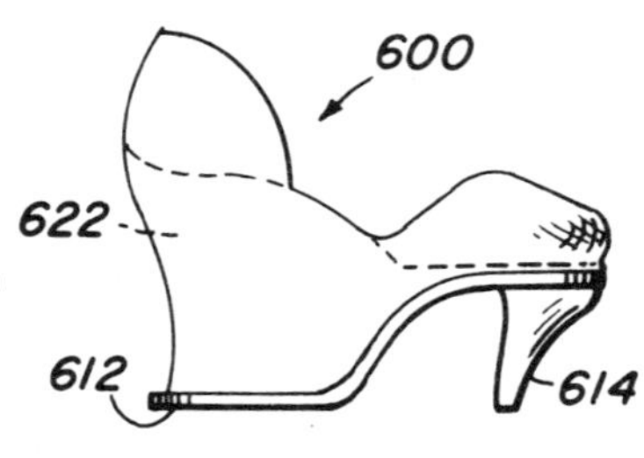

FIG. 6

This shoe fools a pursuer into thinking you are going in the opposite direction.

United States Patent [19] [11] **4,044,482**

Mosch [45] **Aug. 30, 1977**

[54] **WARNING DEVICE**

[76] Inventor: **Alfred Mosch,** 9705 NW. 70 St., Tamarac, Fla. 33321

[21] Appl. No.: **670,351**

[22] Filed: **Mar. 25, 1976**

[51] **Int. Cl.**[2] **B60Q 7/02**

[52] **U.S. Cl.** .... **40/129 C;** 116/28 R

[58] **Field of Search** .... 116/28 R; 40/129 C, 40/134, 130 R; 240/2 R, 7.1 R

[56] **References Cited**

U.S. PATENT DOCUMENTS

2,652,650	9/1953	Helms	40/129 C
3,004,359	10/1961	Pisciotta	40/129 C
3,255,725	6/1966	Von Kreidner	116/28
3,276,416	10/1966	Dirks	116/28 R
3,594,938	7/1971	Mosch	40/129 C
3,761,890	9/1973	Fritts	116/28 R

Primary Examiner—S. Clement Swisher
Assistant Examiner—Denis E. Corr
Attorney, Agent, or Firm—Ernest F. Marmorek

[57] **ABSTRACT**

An optical warning device has a sign that is mounted on the inner surface of the lid of a vehicle compartment, and a light source that illuminates the sign.

8 Claims, 3 Drawing Figures

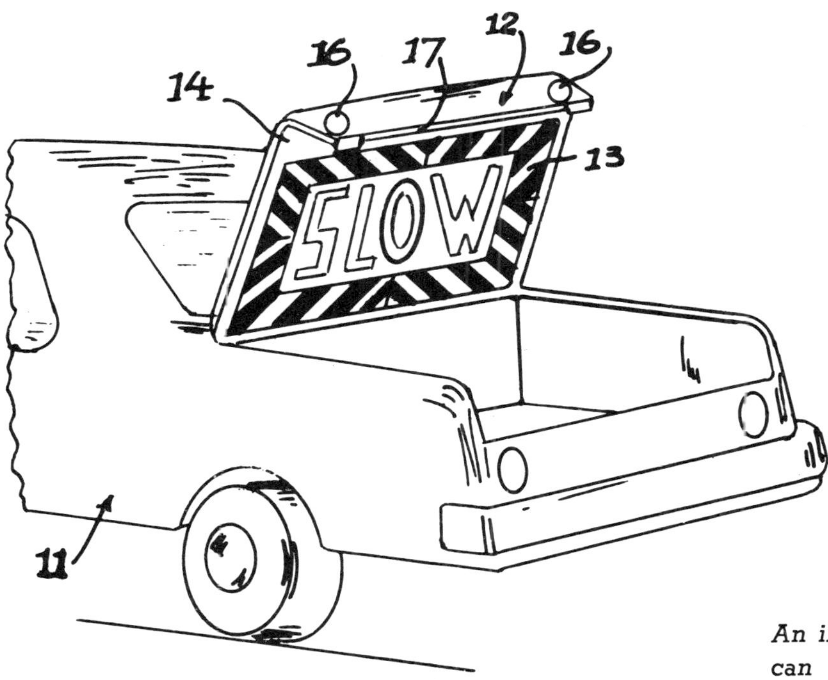

An illuminated warning sign that can be activated by raising the trunk.

United States Patent [19] [11] **4,044,405**
Kreiss [45] **Aug. 30, 1977**

[54] **TARGET IN A BOWL OR URINAL TO ATTRACT THE ATTENTION OF URINATING HUMAN MALES**

[76] Inventor: **Joel S. Kreiss,** Washington Valley Road, Martinsville, N.J. 08836

[21] Appl. No.: **652,816**

[22] Filed: **Jan. 27, 1976**

[51] **Int. Cl.**[2] **A47K 17/00**
[52] **U.S. Cl.** **4/1**
[58] **Field of Search** .... 4/1; 273/127 R, 102 R

[56] **References Cited**

U.S. PATENT DOCUMENTS

2,703,407	3/1955	Henoch et al.	4/1
2,931,047	4/1960	Stebbins	4/1
3,212,104	10/1965	Stevens	4/1

Primary Examiner—Henry K. Artis
Attorney, Agent, or Firm—David S. Woronoff

[57] **ABSTRACT**

A target fixedly connected to a urinal or toilet to attract the attention of human males.

8 Claims, 4 Drawing Figures

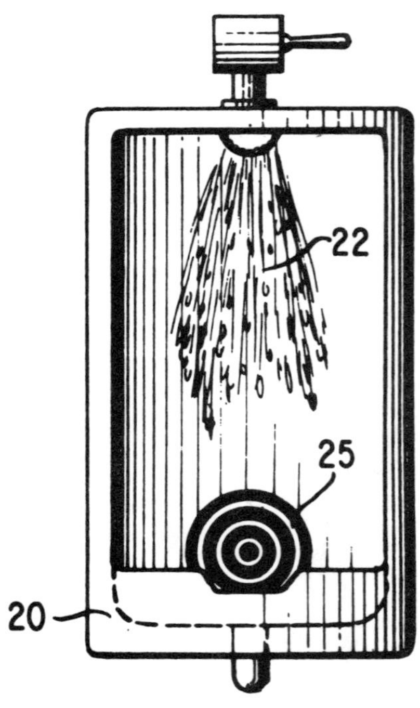

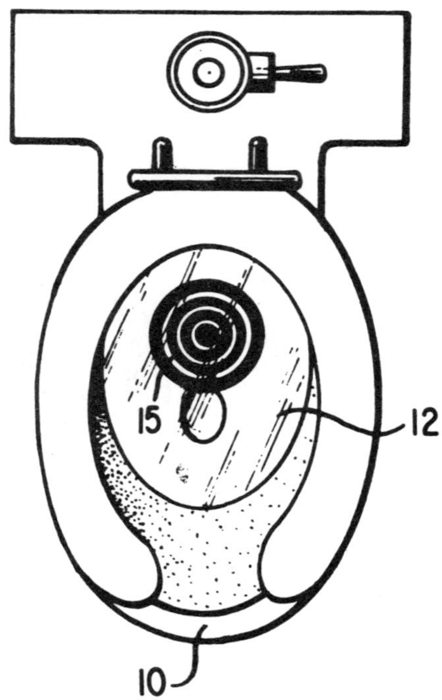

This target is said to be safe, sanitary, and does not require independent cleaning.

Index

Index to Historic Patents